The BeGin

This book is all about the 5th Gear, how to get there and how to stay there, obstacles notwithstanding, facilitators notwithstanding. This book includes a global economic overview, which helps to explain economic cultures in various countries that may serve as good or bad models of economic development, as the reader likes.

This book is a full virtual amalgamation of five different books, 5th Gear, Rear Wiper (a risk management perspective), The BeGin (itself), The Obvious Indian and The Fiction (which is a fictional autobiographical work). This is a far easier, although far more complex task, than handling five different works separately. There are some authors who have written dozens, if not hundreds of novels, and, I can't think why, one or two explaining the pattern of thought would have done quite nicely. Then again Louis L'Amour was an exception, he wrote real stories. Readers are required to spot the separate books and there are surprise prizes (nothing of great value) and recognition (probably of great value) to those who are able to identify all the five books, especially Volume II. The author himself, has tremendous difficulty in consistently identifying Volume II.

The Obvious Indian (hereinafter known simply as TOI), is a collection of observations of an obvious Indian national, the author's second shelf (as opposed to self). This is a powerful book, a book to take on a holiday, and not come back.

A one way Pacific cruise (the Indian Ocean is deeper in parts, however, the Pacific is more scenic and accommodating). The BeGin is every economist's essential text, an expert's dig site and delight, a learner's kaleidoscope.

All estimates, guesstimates and forecasts in this book are the author's own and are covered by the umbrella copyright, which in itself does not mean that they are right.

ISBN: 1-4196-8553-8
ISBN-13: 9781419685538

Visit www.booksurge.com to order additional copies

The Index

This book must BeGin with The Index—The Index cannot be at the end of the book, this is not right at all, nobody uses an index at the end of a book, further, this book does NOT need a table of contents—the reader is advised to read the book in ONE GO. Therefore, in this index, page numbers have not been provided to facilitate progressive reading of ideas, models and cases included in the text.

The author has given below a passage to some key concepts in this book, in no particular order. In between these definitive stylish passages, there are several other chapters and foot note pages that in fact represent, in some instances, partially factual circumstances (as distinguished from grossly inaccurate, this is a term that has been developed by the author, post the USA's strategy of shattering peace in the Middle East):

- China
- USA
- India
- Kuwait
- France—Immigration
- Displaced Economics—10 Blunders of the World
- 5th Gear—UN, IMF, Unemployment Democracy etc.
- International Aid
- Welfare States and Generational Accounting
- Tax Reform
- Forecasts
- The Valuation of Countries

- The Energy Standard
- Carbon Polluters—for some strange reason, industries discharge carbon pollutants into the atmosphere instead of depositing them into the ground. This simple cost effective solution would drop global warming by around 30%, besides helping to accumulate valuable carbon deposits. It is strange that while economies are fueled by the exploitation of carbon reserves, their own carbon pollutants are wastefully discharged into the atmosphere through age old chimney stacks.

Not all chapters/sections/topics are included in this Index. This Index was written before the book—the yolk before the chicken and, its purpose is to develop for the reader the logical progression of ideas.

Not Fiction — Violet Screech

This is a volume about economic development. The theory of economic development has been explained with reference to specific countries with clearly distinguishing economic features. The author has visited these countries in the process of developing and in some instances to confirm theoretical streaks, especially the bluish grayish ones. Reagan had it right, most of the time at least, one must confirm in theory what has worked in practice.

- Kenya
- United States of America

- Kuwait
- India; and
- Australia

Each of these economies has been discussed with reference to matters such as:

- Sustainability
- Social security
- Inflation
- Income levels
- Social integration
- Foreign exchange management

Given below is an indication of the most sustainable economies [of those listed above], humanly and economically, ranking does not reflect or take into account political stability or size of the economy:

1. Kenya
2. India
3. Kuwait
4. United States of America; and
5. Australia

The first file notes are therefore, on Kenya and that is where this volume really screeches off (maybe that should be 'roars'). Note, however, that China is not included above. China is not a sustainable economy, in that sense, or for that matter, in most senses. I am not even sure that China is an economy, China is more a managed society than an economy. China is not free market and is in many ways even more regulated than the USSR ever was or will be (given that Russia is inevitably moving forward to pre USSR type managed production economics). China is a human tragedy already happened with little humanity and much less human rights. It is small wonder then, that China is so comfortable with North Korea. The Chinese model is dependent upon keeping masses of people in abysmal peasantric poverty. Poverty and human misery are the key economic drivers for China. Religious freedom of course does not exist in China but the Chinese businessman does believe in God and in profiting from others' beliefs in God. The Chinese Communist Party is not much of a party—the last time they served fries was when Ping Chin Dhao (pronounced as Pin Dhow—the 'Chin' is silent as are all their people) raided the lost city beneath the seventh wall, or some such non existent event.

Kenya—Safari and Tea

Kenya is a largish country, go look up some stats if you really want to know. The country is blessed with a wonderful climate and is unpolluted industrially (there is perhaps a strong correlation there).

PlusShekaranKumaraswamynathan (referred to hereinafter as 'Ploo' of 'Ploosamy' or as 'Samy') was a genius, a troubled genius. It is only right that his fictional autobiography, therefore, commences only with the period after his retirement, as a government servant, at the age of 58. Ploo was a retired mathematician, who had served for little over 26 years at the GOSIP (governmental statistical institute & provider) in an Asian country. By disposition and physical make up, Ploo was roly, not very poly, had a large thick black moustache, a substantial midriff and curd with rice for lunch, dripping at the elbows. Ploo had an uneventful 26 years with GOSIP. The last 15 of which had been particularly uneventful, since Ploo's job (entire department) had been replaced by a computer, but then nobody noticed much, so Ploo became during that period a whiz at crossword puzzles, while the others in the department took to various other occupations such as knitting, investing on the stock market, supplying biscuits and mince puffs, selling pets etc.

Post retirement, Ploo naturally discovered that solving crossword puzzles on one's own time held no charm at all and certainly did not earn any moolah (as in money, not to be confused with a religious designation). Post retirement, Ploo realized that he must finally have an 'occupation', he could no longer say that he worked in GOSIP or for GOSIP or even indulged in GOSIP. It was important to finally work, now that he had retired. Ploo had sort of looked forward to this, 26 years at GOSIP had sort of got him to the stage of fantasizing about doing real work and he often wondered what it would be like, he had heard of some people in some companies who worked for a living and it sounded so very strange.

So, Ploo, after two months of viewing television serials, decided to become an economic investigator, a detective — naturally his prime methodology would be statistical deduction. The next logical step was then, to look for something to investigate, something to which his formidable statistical crossword solving capabilities could be applied. Ploo had an aptitude and an appetite for this sort of thing, he had explained to his director general, in his very first year on the job, the subtle difference between a regression and a recession and that the two were very different in some countries (such as in India).

With a small investment, Ploosamy, decided to develop his first case in Kenya. So began the lives and times of Ploosamy, the economic detective in Kenya, commencing with the case of the Missing Equator and the case of the Cold Mountain (with sheep...very woolly sheep).

Kenya is largely dependent upon tourist revenues, hordes of them wanting to have a dekho at a lion, hippo, giraffe, elephant or a free roaming radical alligator, with the occasional leopard thrown in. A leopard or panther cub, bye the way, can be the most fearsome little cuddly creature one may encounter for a while on this planet. For wild life, this country is unparalleled, both tourist and animal. The equator runs right through the country and so does the continental divide, like butter through a knife.

Nairobi is the capital city and the most well known, Mombassa is the port city. English is commonly spoken and usually spoken reasonably well. The education system is not particularly great, so this is actually surprising. Some Kenyans get educated overseas, the UK being a favorite. It took Kenyans several years to realize that the future policies of sea faring British citizens would be British jobs for British workers (read 'white' for British). Britain did not have just a racial discrimination system, it had religious discrimination, colored discrimination, age discrimination etc. Discrimination and division were quite well developed as socially divisive forces, something that the British had picked up during their enslaving days in India.

Tea plantations are the other good, green side to Kenya. Attempts to industrialize the country have fortunately failed to come good. The plantations bring refreshing greenery in more ways than one. The exports bring in the greenbacks, the plantations bring in general good climes and the overall health index of Kenyans is therefore above average, barring the incidence of tourist seeded immune deficiencies. The Chinese of course have made their attempt at eating the wild life but it has not been very successful—the Chinese are still busy eating wild life from India and Indonesia, under the impression that this will being them good health and cheer. Tiger's paws, Tiger's bones, Tiger prawns, shark fins, strange ant eaters etc. figure in a richly diversified diet that feeds around

2 billion resident Chinese immigrants. A result of the form of Chinese government is that all Chinese are immigrants in their own land—something like an M&A transaction where the shareholders themselves need a hostile take over process to take over their own company from the management.

Lessons learnt in Kenya, other than those above include early exit of foreign domination through cleverly peaceable means, and an understanding local politic that recognizes that peace is essential to economic progress. The economic model is nice, very nice and sustainable, for a country not deep in resources such as oil, gas and the like. Sunshine and smiles are in abundance. That is, so long as the Chinese are kept to road building gangs and to eating only the smaller dogs.

A demonstration by Kenya, that economic stability, if not prosperity, is entirely possible, even without access to iron, oil, gas, coal, trade routes, advanced technology, large food grain production, military dominance. Is the English language an advantage? It is in this case because of the tourist industry. Is the local trading Indian population an advantage? It is in this case since they are in little position to make presence politically, especially post Uganda, when heads adorned refrigerators. Are natural resources and wild life preserved? Largely, yes, mainly because it is good business to have elephants calving instead of calved elephant ivory.

The food? Wonderful touristic delight for the non vegetarian, varieties from zebra, giraffe, crocodile (you should check up some day the difference between that and an alligator, they differ significantly in taste, especially their taste for humans), and wildebeest (the lion favorite beef like variety). Word of caution 'Jambo' is hello and not elephant, and a 'fucktory' is a (usually very decent) manufacturing plant or enterprise. Security though is not very good after four/five (morning or evening). Kenya has some neighbors that routinely send in some elements that thrive on petty crime and some major. In general, Mombassa is a bit worse off than Nairobi.

Is the local population trustworthy? Largely, yes, once again because they understand the essence of tourism. Are the expatriates trustworthy? Largely, no, even to their own kind. As everywhere else the expatriate is out to make some money, and then, some more. Then save it, and then waste it on trying to immigrate to some degenerate racist western nation, such as USA, UK or Canada (Spain having largely redeemed its reputation with the King asking Hugo to shut up—something that George Bush had never quite dared to achieve).

Plooswamy, never did solve his first case—the case of the Missing Equator, in a way, since he did discover that it wasn't in fact all that missing...in fact it was THERE (and still is). Ploo's experience standing at the equator was in his own words 'awesome'....it felt for the umpteenth time that the world revolved around him....and a couple of four legged vertically striped zebras that idly watched him stand there. It felt as if his moustache would drop off the end of the earth and waft down into the southern hemisphere, he could even feel a touch of cold air from the Antar(c)tica on his moustache.

Several hippo, giraffe and toothy crocodile sightings later and after encountering much wild life (the two legged variety), Ploo uncovered the mystery of the Cold Mountain (and the woolly sheep). Sheep provided wool, the farmers provided the wool to local garment manufacturers or exporters (local exporters as opposed to export exporters). It just did not add up statistically. Now here was a case to thrill the most hardened Poirotical Marplenian Sherlockian, Home-sickan detective. After months of studying the problem on Cold Mountain, Ploo realized that the sheep were actually capable of producing much less wool than the wool being processed in Kenya (even allowing for lint—not that anybody took wool out of a sheep's belly button) and that Kenyan processors and traders were using much more wool, than they should, given norms for such processing. So, Plooswamy decided to study the situation—carefully, very carefully, it was fraught with dangerous draught.

What he then discovered through patient observations at banks and chats with bank managers was quite simply that a fairly good percentage of payments for wool were in fact not made to farmers, but were withdrawn in cash by processing units themselves. One banker remarked idly "Why do you say the fucktory manager should not draw the wool payments? He be friend with the farmer, after they be eight but before they be eleven". Ploo looked like he had been just hit for a home run by his Iranian Persian cat.

The stunning earth shattering deduction, off the equator, was that this wool purchased was in fact not wool purchased, but cash drawn by processors, not for wool purchases. Ploo was now laboring under a crushing disadvantage. Wool processing was not a 'focus' industry in Kenya, coffee and tourism on the other hand, were focus industries and did not in fuckt need investments in fucktories. Ploo spent a second year, diligently applying himself to the problem of what happened to the wool purchases, that were in fact not wool purchases. He arrived at a multitude of answers, namely, payments to local politicians, payment to national politicians, payments to international politicians, take home payments to processing unit managers, take home payments to processing unit owners and white laundering of illegally earned income (declared in the farmer's hands—nobody would exert enough energy to prove that sheep were not really producing that amount of wool!!—for one it was too tedious an exercise, and for another, there were too many gratuitous participants in the scheme). The fucktories of course showed losses on the excess purchases of wool and did not have to pay taxes.

This left Ploo in a soup. After two years of painstaking investigation, Ploo had solved his first economic mystery case. The food had been super, the weather excellent and the local people most hospitable and warmly welcoming. Ploo, had a case, he had the solution—but he was in a soup—nobody wanted the case and even less, the solution. Some diligent enquiries uncovered a sad truth, if Ploo did disclose his information, he could only end up either as croc or lion dinner (somehow he had never seen either one of them having lunch at noon). Plooswamy left Kenya a sad but wiser man. He felt in many ways like Livingstone or Columbus—he had discovered another economy, thick in the undergrowth, luxuriant in its spread and growth and quietly reported as economic inefficiencies of the farming sector and fuck-tory sector!! There was however, a silver lining, he was given a warm send off at the airport by a motley collection of bankers and farmers and politicians—and an assortment of gifts - bouquets, coffee pots, monkey's teeth, monkey's tail, elephant's teeth (teeth not tusks, teeth of elephants are much rarer, some even say they do not exist) and the beard of a lion (painstakingly cut during a lion's visit to the local hair dressing saloon). They were happy that Ploo had kept their secret and had left things undisturbed—for Ploo it was a simple matter—he had the satisfaction of solving his economic mystery and he had kept his skin intact. This, in fact, is the real reason, why there are no drums in the Masai Mara, covered with Ploo skin, till today.

I hear, now, that up in Cold Mountain, super fine wool, is referred to as Ploo or Samy, especially the variety that is so 'superfine' that is cannot be seen. Poor Ploo, had he been an accountant, would have realized on his first visit to Nairobi, that no accountant or auditor, ever audited the 'wool purchases' account…clearly everybody knew that there were more sheep back of Cold Mountain.

Has the average Kenyan seen a tiger? No, wouldn't even know what a tiger is, first reaction is that it must be a country, if not, a large prawn in China. Has the average Thai seen a lion? No, maybe heard of one.

Is it awesome to stand on the equator? Yes, awesome and chilly sometimes. Kenya favors lower temperatures and the golf is quite good in parts, very scenic. The log huts at El Doret and the Safari at Mara Serena are simply great. The carrots are really orange and the peas are really green, the showers work, the hot water rolls in nicely and the lion yawns gamely, on request…(by the lioness). In lionical society, it is the lady lioness who calls the yawns. The lion's job description includes yawns and roars on demand.

There is a Catholic population and church service is traditional. This is clearly a saving grace for a country that is otherwise racked by the ills of tourism and takes Kenya one step closer to Goa (west coast idyllic location—India), including the reddish caked mud and the sloping landscape.

Contrast Kenya with the rest of Africa, including the South and the comparison is quite frightening. The reasons, political, social and geographic are quite irrelevant to the economic model. Coffee, tea or me? This is a workable economic model, well managed by messy global standards. This is an admirable demonstration of the principle of comparative advantage. This very principle is amply demonstrated in software education in Armenia, medical education in Romania, Bulgaria, industrial output in Poland and mineral exploitation in Kazakhstan etc. Kenyans are also very uncomplicated with regard to religion and that is a huge help.

The Hunt for Zimbabwe

Africa after the Middle East is the largest conflict zone globally. That is because the fight for Africa is spread between China, France, UK and the USA with France and South Europe generally pitching in for the pickings. The battle has swung noticeably in favor of China, with a majority of the population realizing that China has a security and economic model that works. France and the UK have been at it for a long time and the USA most recently in Sudan and earlier in Egypt. However, they have failed on both the security and economic fronts. Africa is a continent rich in mineral and natural resources. Hydro generated power can rid the continent of energy shortages. Africa has suffered from the western policy of divide and rule, divided (as in Pakistan, Bangladesh, Serbia, Croatia, Kurdistan) into economically dependent, disastrous units that will perpetually be unstable and dependent (on Western aid and Western AIDS).

Zimbabwe has been the centre stone of this conflict for the past few years, the stoning pillar as it were. This is now the centre piece of the economic chess board in Africa. All forces and institutions, including the venerable IMFed etc. are ranged on one side. The battle for Zimbabwe and DRC will determine to a large extent who controls the vast natural resources of Africa. Africa, like India needs to be welded into a large single country (not necessarily democracy). India was splintered into many 'Maharajah' states until nationalistic political elements came together to form a country within the prison of British rule. With global warming, Africa is also the best land mass for humans into the 21ˢᵗ century. Of course the US of A will probably realize that only by 2010, by which time the UK would have been regularly swamped by floods.

The African continent, from north west to the south eastern tip, is rich in resources of every hue and kind. One might be tempted to say that Africa together with the marshes of Iraq was the original garden of Eden. I am quite sure that Mandrake, Lothar (many under estimate the role of Lothar) and Phantom would agree whole heartedly. What is the President of Zimbabwe doing? The country's allocation of resources is in the process of being restructured in a major economical-surgical effort. This is critical structural surgery, not merely cosmetic. There is bound to be pain. What has added to the pain is the dramatic opposition from Western nations (who would like to color the situation as a racist/ethnic conflict), including the use of institutions such as the IMFed and the UN. The UN itself has taken the role of the High Priestess of nothingness (classic is Bunkum Hi Moan), administering nothing for the benefit of nothing and providing a voice in the wilderness, remaining largely critical of all independent developmental efforts that are unsupported by either the UK or the US. The leaders of Zimbabwe and Venezuela are taking bold surgical steps to set right economic imbalances. That course of action does not please Western nations whose wealth depends on creating economic dependencies.

It was about the time of the third true reign of the third true President, that Canadian Hookey decided to invest in Zimbabwe ('Zimby' as he liked to call it and therefore, how it shall be referred to hereinafter). Canadian Hookey (known for some strange reason as 'CK' not as 'CH") was a tired old man (most old men are 'tired', unless they are authors). CK was of an indeterminate age, having lived a long time, some time ago, a few years back. CK lives no longer and this little note explains how this state of affairs came to be. CK was basically a farmer and he discovered that the line of distinction between merchant, smuggler and trader, was basically a little matter of taxes and laws. The products were the same bunch, the circumstances and the borders were different.

CK lived in Zimby for 17 years. He was of Canadian origin, he knew there was money in Zimby and for long had promised himself that he would stay there for a couple of years and make some of that money his own and then return to Tungarlee (his village up there—at least he like to call it that—I don't really know if that was the correct name). Very unlike Ploo's farmers of Cold Mountain, CK was a farmers' farmer. That is to say, CK farmed. He owned a farm, and dogs, pigs, sheep, couple of rangy looking ponies, ducks, goats, cows, asses (could have been donkeys) and chicken. CK was at peace, the farm also allowed him cover to trade in just about anything, every side of the border. CK, however, drew the line at animal excrement, that is something he had enough of and would not trade in, not something to be 'inventoried' as he described it.

The political landscape however changed and with time CK realized that the piece of the pie (his pie or cannelloni) wasn't getting any nearer. He had to have a solution. He didn't have much cash, his wife (twice removed/divorced) had taken his credit cards, his credit and his children. Court orders said that Canadian Hookey had to be on a continent other than the one currently in use by his spouse or children (his wife was willing to go to Charles Taylor to enforce and Charles Taylor was a man to be dreaded—he was friendly with the French). CK ran the gamut of schemes to keep him afloat and alive. Zimby was a tough place back then. CK once tried to rob a bank and then realized a few sad truths, Zimby banks did not have money, Zimby banks had already been robbed, all Zimby robbers knew each other, all Zimby bankers knew all Zimby robbers, Zimby robbers were Zimby depositors. That course of action was, therefore, sadly, ruled out. Somebody had seen it all, done it all and already plundered it all to take back home. There had to another way or ways.

CK had a friend—Kanengo. Kanengo was the very antithesis of CK. Where CK was short and pudgy with small distrustful Chinaman eyes, Kanengo was tall, lanky, broad shouldered, wide forehead, long flowing locks, tied back with a dirty head band (Im not sure whether it was dirty or whether it was just a brown head band—but there were serious doubts). Kanengo was an honest government official and this is where CK did not see eye to eye with him—the 'honest' part. Honesty and ethics made CK afraid, some people are afraid of the dark, even as a child, CK had always been afraid of honesty and ethics.

CK with some help from Kanengo pulled off one of the wildest money plundering schemes in the history of Zimby. It all ended rather sadly for CK. CK was given a fitting burial in Tungarlee, in true monarchial tradition for the honored, 21 spears thrown at him as he was lowered into the pit, tar dripped gently over, and then set on fire. Naturally, the IMF, UKF, USF and other F's were most displeased and promptly protested—Kanengo later said that he had received several formal letters protesting the quality of tar used.

What was Canadian Hookey's plan, where did it succeed? where did it fail? Did it in fact fail? Did Canadian Hookey in fact want to live? These were some of the questions that troubled Plooswamy when the case was first introduced to him.

Ploo was, by now, a celebrated monk (ey) in the region and was looked up to get to the bottom of such dreadful questions and matters, without getting himself to the bottom of the river (that's where the crocs were, the surface was not so bad with the hippos).

CK, it turns out had long since realized that his farm was never going to make him a pot of money, eggs, milk and chickens notwithstanding in a country of avid meat eaters. He had something good to sell, always, the trouble was CK just could not find somebody willing to pay. Finding somebody capable of paying was the first part of the problem, the second more difficult part of the problem was finding, from that small population (Oh, sooo small) a person *willing* to pay. For what could be had for free, why would a wise one pay? And one had to be wise to be able to pay. There is was, the basic ground level economic mystery paradox—a wise man had the ability to pay but was wise enough not to pay. "This is it pal Kanengo" CK moaned "It's the end of the line, this train's lost off the tracks, its either me or the bullet, I cant go on anymore, promise me you'll look after Mangy (the red pony)". Kanengo smiled "Not for nothing there bees so mannees Pharohs buried in Afreeka, you see, I give you plan".

And, so it was Kanengo who discovered a way, quite accidentally, playing oligopolistic monopsony with his 11 year old grandson (never mind how Kanengo who was at the time 46 could have a 11 year old grandson—that's really really complicated territory). CK surrendered his land, only his land, to the local governmental authority, for an irrigation project. This was the master Kasporovian stroke, the dreaded poisoned pawn, the dreaded variation. Nobody, but nobody, knew what to do with surrendered land. So Kanengo, and colleagues decided that since the government could not accept a donation from CK—CK should be compensated. Since it was a surrender, CK was paid in cash, half the market monetary value of the land.

But CK, continued to occupy the land, since the government could not provide him with an alternative place of stay, Canadian Hookey continued his farming on the surrendered land. However, irrigation projects need to be implemented, even in the driest of countries, and such projects need to irrigate, even if there is no water. To facilitate the diversion and bottling of a small branch of a river, some 'spade-ground' work had to be done. This meant employment, this was good, since Kanengo and his friends project managed the employment and the work. CK was a happy participant in the spoils at this stage too—significant spoils, since the spade work took up the better part of three years and over 15,000 man days (ok, ok, human days). In fact on many days, the work carried on late into the night, so there was a overtime paid, a lot of overtime, really really a lot. The government had to irrigate and to irrigate one had to dig and here was poor CK surrendering his land to irrigate.

Eventually, three years and 15,000 human days later, the land was prepared to irrigate—but by then the river had dried and Kanengo cried—with happiness. Since that meant that he had to extend the work on the land for another 11 miles (Kanengo was good at squeezing out every advantage—he could have been a tax collector—he measured the distance in miles, not kilometers and for good measure, capped it at the higher of his eldest grandson's age. The 11 miles story could not be stretched very far, people were getting wise and the work was completed within eight months and 11 days.

The water was finally ready to roll, but there was still that little problem of finding a place for CK to live in. CK quietly obtained compensation for his cows, chicken, asses, goats, pigs, ducks, their multiple families and the like. He kept the ponies and his dogs. Since no suitable accommodation could be found for a patriot who had surrendered his land, CK was put up in the nearest town hotel, occupying the entire first floor with four large rooms and a large room to meet visitors. Canadian Hookey was by now something of a local celebrity, having spread during the past three years, or having been a cause of spread, of much notes and resulting great cheer all around. Almost anybody who was anybody had been employed on Canadian Hookey's Tungarlee project (either in name or in reality). The ponies were appropriately stabled and the dogs—well dogs are dogs and they went where they pleased, content to feed at the inn below and occupy the largest of CK's rooms. There was however, among the dogs, a little Chihuahua who mysteriously disappeared and some one swore that the Monday lamb stew had a special flavor to it. The total amount received by CK had by now far surpassed the market value of the land (not that there were any buyers—remember the wise men?) prior to this happy sequence of events. Kanengo then did the unthinkable (he still laments this decision, many years after the loss of his friend). And in retrospect, this was the undoing of the plot, the plot thickened and the thickining was terrible. Kanengo made CK a Zimby (citizen!!). This was shocking and a tactical error. CK could now be a politician himself!! He now longer needed Kanengo, or thought he did not. CK then sought government land and developed a 'national' (it was hara-kiri to call it 'international') veterinary hospital—for abandoned farm animals, principal among which were his own. Canadian Hookey secured land for the project and a government subsidy payable per cow, chicken, pig, dog, ass (animal), and duck that was 'rescued', some say that the project at one stage even profited from international funding.

Kanengo disconnected—animals were for eating—not profiting—goats in particular were tasty (although he had to admit that the Chihuahua left a peculiar taste), and to make matters worse, CK was by now a fairly wealthy land owner, and all by surrendering his land. But CK was a citizen, a patriot, an irrigator and an animal lover. You did not get much thicker than that with the government (here I must add, as author, that in Zimby they use the much preferred 'boss', whereas in India they use 'gormint'—nothing to do with some of their politicians looking like gorillas who have not shaved in a millennium.

Kanengo took to campaigning against CK. The land was black and so could not be owned by a white—nobody could argue with that. CK had cheated the government and Kanengo. He had been broke when Kanengo first met him, and now had more chickens than he then had eggs. But this was not easy, CK had irrigated, he had watered and he had saved animals, he had surrendered his land (the ultimate sacrifice).

It was Kanengo then, who decided with Makenumbo (his second grandson, who was then 11 years old) that CK should truly be given a piece of his land—permanently. CK was invited to a party and a solemn tyre was placed around his neck and gently lit (some silly person had filled the tyre with diesel—Kanengo rather preferred the premium lead free gasoline). CK was then pushed into the pit and tar was gently dripped over him and then the tar was set on fire, somewhere along the way, the spears thrown in for flavor. Kanengo, Makenumbo and the other grandsons wept dearly for CK and later feasted on his goats, cows, chickens, pigs and ducks.

The key question remaining un answered, was where were Kanengo's children? Why was he always with grandsons? Where were his sons? Kanengo, Plooswamy discovered had lost his children, in the span of three years, they were the few who had genuinely worked on the irrigation project. Plooswamy was deeply puzzled, what could one make of all this from a pure economic perspective. He had un covered the facts of the matter but not the riddle. Was Canadian Hookey an economic driver? An entrepreneur? A politician? His income and the income printed and distributed to Kanengo and families, was it part of the GDP? Was the land irrigated to any useful purpose? Did the land in fact have any useful purpose? Why did Canadian Hookey have to be given citizenship? One thing was certain—he had died of natural causes—under the circumstances his death was quite predictable and very very natural. Reminded him of the case of the cricket coach who died of natural causes in the midst of a world cup—'natural' being the operative word. Anyways, just goes to prove that one man's farm could be another man's bee hive.

None of these riddles were ever solved. Ploo was smarter, he had learnt...he had learnt to keep his skin irrevocably attached to the rest of his body and away from crocodiles and leopards. Till today, few people, except the grandson of Makenumbo (who is now 11 years old) know why the town is called Tungarlee C.K.(Tungarlee was the first brand of tooth brush that CK had bought on his arrival in Mistakena, 44 years earlier). A small board on the dusty road 'Tungarlee C.K.' marks the location of the irrigation project—a duck pond in the midst of nowhere, the ducks quacking, asking the same question always 'what the heck are we doing here'? Till to-day there aren't any frogs in Tungarlee C.K. pond, it just isn't deep enough. Ploosamy had solved his second economic mystery, once again with a solution that nobody wanted. The stage was ripe for forming the MEOWs (Major Economic Offence Wing)

United States of America

The USA is a large economy with a not so surprising hollow-ness. In the US of A when people go on a diet, they first lose weight from the inside, at least this is what somebody like Opera may tell them. Then again, to lose weight a number of people in the US of A repeatedly visit their 'shrink' and that is why practicing psychiatry is such good business in the US. This is a young country with a remarkably failed currency, legal system, corporate governance system, political system and economic model (all failed, but not necessarily in that order), in stark contrast with some of the so called developing countries. "The political system" Ploo noted with some amuse-ment "is sooo obviously failed if the prime candidate is a 60 year old thin shouldered bow legged woman with a sneer-ing lopsided grin, who prances around the election platform, waving her arms around like a female Don Quixote or like a school marm at an animal farm, while saying one thing and voting the other way on every major issue".

Consider that the USA is unable to effectively meet the challenges posed by a relatively small population. Unemployment, lack of savings, huge trade and budgetary deficits , together with the inability to effectively meet the obligations of a stuttering health care and retirement benefit system, characterize an economic model that is as outdated as it is ill.

The USA has several major weaknesses. Principal among them being the faded education system. The education system encourages poor academic effort and dysfunctional student behavior. Most students are not convinced after years of schooling that the pen is mightier than the barrel. It is also beyond the affordable means for a large proportion of the population, and therefore, encourages dysfunctional behavior of parents—leading to completely dysfunctional families. College is a distant dream for the majority, unlike most developing countries. This has left the USA standing in the dust cloud of developing countries that either export large numbers of qualified professionals or take back from the USA jobs to their home markets, thus compounding the unemployment problem of the USA. As Ploo exclaimed "What can you say when the Secretary is called Dr. Rice and has not actually eaten rice for over 25 years?"

The tax system has proven that it will never meet either the fiscal or social needs of a demanding society. The outmoded tax framework has as many constructive loopholes as a cement sieve (I must confess that I am not entirely sure what exactly this is, but is sounded so nice) and has driven the collection volumes down over time.

The external debt at the rate of domestic savings, is the equivalent of 450+ years of income and savings for the current population, in fact 457 years, without allowance for interest.

Just about the only aspect of the economic model that had held up for a while was the transportation system, based on a system of distributed private transport and air travel. However, in recent years, the air travel mode has proven, in the USA, to be cost ineffective and just another burden on the economy. The vast majority has not realized the full benefits of rail travel and trudges through a series of automatic cars that guzzle fuel at horrifying rates. Water based transportation modes and water based connectivity has not been developed although that is probably the most efficient system after the stage coach (without the stage coaches' propensity for hold ups—known in SOX terminology as inherent risk).

The USA economic and social model has proven sustainable only at population levels of around 250 million, beyond which the stress on the model tends to develop fissures and cracks in the super structure. This is truly astonishing given the abundance of natural resources, and smacks of gross mismanagement induced by a succession of Presidents who have shown an all too unhealthy interest in interns. The USA today is saddled with enormous problems of a huge trade deficit, huge budgetary deficits, inability to fund health care and retirement benefit plans, an ineffective tax system etc.

The corporate governance structure of the USA and the regulatory mechanisms, have failed in a dominoistic manner, that through imperfect imitation has caused bunkers of problems in developing countries, especially those who have shifted from the relatively safe, risk averse confines of the British system, to the adventurous USA regulatory and capital market mechanisms. It is clear that the financial markets in the USA are characterized, not by a spirit of entrepreneurship but by a spirit of adventurism and there is an essential dividing line or two between these. This dividing line/s is not fine, it is clear and bold and large. USA has consciously as a country, as a society, chosen the spirit of adventurism as its founding principle of financial markets and monetary systems. Now, entrepreneurship, risk taking and white water rafting (adventurism) are not to be co mingled and confused as economic policy. The average American citizen does not understand that government and personal loans need to be repaid, not refinanced.

The USA's economic model is currently hurtling downward through bankruptcy at asteriodical pace, churning through in its wake other dollar dependent economies. Is there nothing therefore good to be said of the capitalistic, productionalistic economic base? There is, actually. The disastrous downward spiral may be arrested through an effective combination of a larger role for the government in running businesses, through a reversal of privatization, and also a reduction in the dependency of the economy on core producing areas. The other peaceable means of halting the catastrophic charge to the cliff edge is of course splitting the country into more than one independent autonomous country states. This has some political disadvantages, but none apply to the current situation in which the USA finds itself. Typically, if the USA were looking at itself, as another independent country, it would suggest splitting the country (as in Yugoslavia, Iraq, SE Asia etc.) into smaller manageable countries.

The vast destruction of the small town economy (has to be seen to be believed) and the evaporationism of the rural economic framework has lent a non dynamic instability to the fiscal and economic and resource employment framework. It is in developing countries that the word 'rural' is used, in the USA they call it the 'farm' sector and refuse to acknowledge the village economy, the Brits acknowledge the village economy, but think it is something cute and quaint, a matter of pride, not a matter of failing economics. The USA has a Christian economic model driven by the charity of the Jewish business community (as distinguished from that of the Jewish people). The USA has in the past (and continues) exported economic, political and social insecurity and instability. This is perhaps the core role of a world power, the same with the Greeks, Egyptians, Romans, the British and now the USA (the USSR was never really a world power in that sense). World powers use their capital resources to develop dependency relationships with countries by weakening their economic and social fabric—this is what the USA is still attempting in SE Asia and in the ME. The truth hurts always, but the truth is one—ask Benny, as Ploo would say.

In short, Chris Columbi or somebody else needs to discover the Americas once again. South America of course has the discarded economic genetics of the North. Poor Canada essentially suffers from the same afflictions, the saving grace for Canada, being the oil sands that are viable at $80 a barrel. Canada should unplug its economy from the economic grid south of the border. The currency and health-elder care system (Hil Bil Clinton notwithstanding) of the USA are destined to go the Niagra way.

It is however, as difficult to reduce the importance of the US dollar, as it is to reduce the importance of the English language.

It was in this spirit of demolition premonition that Plooswamy stepped in. Having had his fill of adventure (and having profited from such adventure) in Africa (Zimby and Kenya), Ploo decided that he could invest a couple of years in the USA, after all he was now 64 and if he did not visit the USA before he was 68 (bad things happen at 68, ask anybody who remembers Vietnam), he was convinced that he would never. Ploo had worked out a way of settling into the USA that would permit him to carry on his suo motto investigations, undisturbed. During his stay in the USA, Ploo would work at an adult education centre at night teaching mathematics, and for three hours at a zoo caring for wild animals from the East during the afternoons, that sort of left him (and the animals) free in the mornings. An old colleague of his (actually, at this point all his colleagues were old) was a senior research associate at the University of Bikago, involved in some weather beaten economic projects that nobody wanted to touch. One of these projects allowed Kid Rangy (his name was

Kediarathan Ranganathan and he had long since given up using his name—anyway 'Kid Rangy' was more economical) to recruit specialist consultants on the research teams, for specific durations and for specific projects. This likeable project (that made all the other projects worth while for the Kid) addressed an old problem—whether large corporations helped small businesses or whether it was the other way around and small businesses in fact supported large corporations.

The Kid was an interesting person to work with. He justified Ploo's appointment on the ground of his extensive post retirement experience in Africa with small businesses. Ploo was contracted by the Kid in a much budgeted for position, to look into the matter and promptly settled into the task, after clarifying that Wacker Drive was not Whacky Drive. Kid Rangy was aware that Ploo, despite his formidable capabilities would need some help. Kid Rangy therefore, pulled in another old horse, Dumpy Carthwright who was second economist to CD Windsor. Ploo passed the first month in bliss with Dumpy, both having budgets to blow and sampled local Chinese take outs every evening (not to be confused with Chinese hand outs). Ploo and Dumpy even took in a theater performance, visited China Town and rode the Lines. It was December and it was the time of the year that Ploo was especially restless. Restless to do something to get the project moving. In a marathon meeting at the University, Plooswamy, Dumpy Carthwright and Kid Rangy named the project— Project SuperAnnuation. It was a queer name but it met all their objectives. Dumpy just wanted to use the word 'Super', Kid Rangy (the budget allocator) wanted a name that nobody would really question in a list of allocations and Ploo wanted to use the word 'annual' or a variation, to remind him that he had to finish the project within a year (he did not want to spend another chilly winter in Bikago across those very large ice pools called lakes (it was easy to understand why some people living on either side of the lakes were called Lakers).

Ploo, Dumpy and the Kid selected three businesses to study—a soda pop distributor, a drug manufacturer and a jewelry shop. That should be enough and covered a decent enough spectrum, besides providing enough work for the next 11 months. The objects of study were naturally chosen from the business connections of teaching staff (some University Bikago staff actually had productive duties) and therefore, information was easily accessible. Everybody wanted to participate in the study, it was a bit like juror duty, without the problem of having to find somebody guilty or not...Dumpy always thought that 'not' was better, everybody liked their freedom and anyways he hated judges and wardens.

The soda pop distributor was owned by a large black woman, had thirty employees, driving vans and reported a profit. Kid Rangy was a happy man, easy case, case closed, big business helped small business, minority employs majority, minority makes small profit (big profit would not have been good—that's what made the US-Ass unhappy about Iraq and Iran, the Kid remembered just in time). Dumpy had to be a spoilt sport. He refused to close the file. About this time, Ploo decided to take a vacation and the Kid promised him that nobody at Bikago would notice, so Ploo went off on a two year vacation. Ploo later added 11 days to those two years, but nobody noticed that either.

Dumpy Carthwright was a tall thin, reed-ish sort of man with red-ish sort of hair and a pair of spectacles that urgently, always needed pushing up the bridge (his bridge, not bridges generally). Dumpy had a receding hairline ('had'—because now he doesn't have any crowning hair left) and a thin, small, soda straw like moustache, with needlepoint waxed edges. Dumpy swore (often) that if he ever needed a blood test done, he could do it with the ends of his moustache. That particular boast was tested many years later, in Columbia, but that's a different story. Dumpy was a cynic, the original cynic and also an opportunist—a cynical opportunist who cycled and therefore, was a cyclical, cynical opportunist. Dumpy enlisted the help of Cration Weathersome to review the soda pop distributor (SPD)—why was the SPD in fact making money? Why was the minority making money ? and, more importantly, at whose' expense?

For, Carthwright and Cration had a pet common theory (as distinguished from common pets i.e. white mice and Persian cats), that is somebody if making money, some other person or firm is losing it, unless it is the government who just goes ahead and prints it!! Both were also convinced that beneath every surface business model, there was an underlying undiscovered business model, for every cash generating business. Dumpy was shocked to find that the large black woman, was just large, not large and fat—most large

people tend to be fat, and this was a statistical outlier (don't forget that Ploo's economic criminal methodologies were being firmly put to the test). Five months of pain staking research (and having eaten many many stakes) later—Kid said 'well done' (the research, not the stakes). The large black thin woman, Bonaventura Dieasa (BD) who owned the SPD, actually presented several interesting insights into how an SPD could make money.

To cut a long story short:

- BD was not the real owner of the SPD
- The SPD barely made its bank payments
- The SPD made money for BD and the owner on the delivery van purchases and sales (the delivery van company had a friendly executive—this is where BD came in, BD kept the executive friendly—both were members of the same floriculture club)
- The SPD delivery vehicles did not deliver only soda
- The SPD delivery vehicles also collected 'stuff' on the round trip, the second leg of the trip being made between 11 pm and 1 am
- BD and the owner made a bundle on the SPD deal with the soda manufacturer
- The owner of the SPD was the bank manager
- BD was not black—only black on paper at the bank—a blank black at the bank
- BD did not really have thirty employees on the SPD payroll—only six cops—but then, they took the payroll of thirty minimum wage—maximum effort employees.

But the soda pop was good and the cash was rolling in and it was a successful small business. Ploo was happy to hear the good news (they hadn't after all taken the tempting soda straw view), economic fraud apparently existed on the continent. Ploo (still on vacation), Dumpy and the Kid decided as in the earlier cases, not to do anything, i.e. not to squeal,

Cration Weathersome was worried some about this, he had this 'ethics' thing but the axis of economic evil discoverers convinced CW that there was actually nobody, but nobody, who required them to disclose. Their job was economic research, they weren't an economic offender wing (anyway the EOWs were functioning more like MEOWs).

Ploo, who by now, had acquired the considerable admiration and respect (two entirely different things) of his team (Cration had been inducted and was enjoying the proceedings—and the University of Bikago was bank rolling), urged his friends (term used here in a loose fashion) to pursue the case of the drug manufacturer.

Cration begged to be team leader on this one. "I cant very well sit by the pool like you" Cration moaned to Ploo "I need some action to keep these old bones moving". Ploo agreed, in any case, he was on vacation and CW did not seem like the kind of researcher who would call up at 3 am (or even 3 pm). CW was a bit more inspired than the Kid and it was during one of his coffee breaks that he came up with the idea of actually doing an economic research paper for the University of Bikago—anyway they were paying for it—so CW recruited 11 students to actually study some of Ploo's notes and prepare sensible economic research papers that the University could use to prepare uncorrupted students of economics for the real world—it was a bit like learning the complexities of chess openings by reversing the moves of a grandmaster.

CW decided to meet the drug manufacturer with the Kid. The Kid anyway, had a sweet tooth and liked his bacon too (sunny side up, with poached eggs). The Kid had in fact invented sunny side up bacon—but that story is told in his adventures in La Complaba. Dumpy meanwhile, decided to join Ploo on his vacation, after all, if one could, why couldn't two? The drug manufacturer was a drug manufacturer, a third party contracting site for a large corporation. A honest to goodness FDA (feared, despised adversary) cleared business with no complaints from consumers, large corporation, employees, in fact no complaints from anybody who did not have a stake in the business. The only person who did have a stake in the business was Shaolin. That wasn't his real name, but he was called Shaolin because he was of Chinese origin, Chinese nationality and a sixth generation illegal Chinese immigrant, who had over stayed six generations.

Shaolin's real name was Wan Zee Glue (I'm not so sure about the family name since Ploo wrote this down while at the beach and the manuscript had a bit of something on it—but it sounded like 'Glue' and could easily have been 'Blue'). Anyway, WZG was a nice man with a large family, WZG had 11 children and three wives—he always maintained as an atheist he could have as many wives as he wanted, since he did not hold any particular orthodox or un orthodox religious beliefs. This made the situation very interesting since neither Ploo, Dumpy Carthwright, Cration Weathersome or Kediarathan Ranganathan (the Kid) had ever, ever encountered somebody who did not have religious beliefs. They found it truly incredible that in this day and age of scientific and technological advance, there was actually somebody who did not acknowledge the existence of the creator. God was a proven fact, in God we trust and God supports the US dollar—surely everybody knew that—therefore, there was obviously a God. Some Chinese, however, especially the immigrants, were mistakenly under the impression that the global currency was noodles (medium spicy) and curry (spicy).

WZG had a factory (note the use of the more conventional 'factory') that manufactured encapsulated medicines, with formulations provided by the corporation (hereinafter called 'the corporation C'). The unit filled, closed, packaged and distributed to distributors over 43 trillion capsules a year, filled with formulations supplied by the C. WZG's unit received a processing charge that covered his investment in machines, payroll costs, distribution costs and provided him with a reasonable profit. So far so good, a perfectly normal, Carthwrightian situation, definitely not Plooastic. Ploo lost interest, anybody who processed 43 trillion capsules a year clearly did not have time for anything else and just had to be the genuine article. The only problem was that this was Cration's first case as team leader and he was not willing to let go. Ploo had once seen a neighborhood dog desperately scramble a hole for a non existent rat and CW's efforts reminded him of that (the dog was eventually hauled away by the dog catchers, and the rat continued to live happily ever after in another hole).

This case was entirely different from the case of BD who managed the SPD. WZG actually was a Chinese who owned the capsule manufacturing unit, and he wasn't large and yellow, even on paper. The capsule manufacturing unit produced and distributed capsules, there were no complaints from the FDA. WZG had never been to Shaolin, but that could hardly be considered an economic crime, or a crime of any nature seeing that even the Shaolin Temple wasn't quite in Shaolin.

So, WZG was profitable, cash profitable and had 11 children, three wives, 43 trillion capsules annually and was an atheist who was called Shaolin but had never been to Shaolin. This was hardly a satisfying summary of the situation and CW was clearly unhappy. There simply had to be a shadow business model, the false profit (aka known in some Jewish circles as the false prophet—but then the Jews called all prophets false—the more peace they preached, the more false they had to be—they were right about Hitler though, he was quite false—even his teeth), the problem was finding it.

WZG may not have been to Shaolin, but he was inscrutable, that is, in CW's words, he could not really be screwed. CW needed help and went back to Bonaventura Dieasa (BD). BD after all, had proven expertise in this sort of thing—one needed a profiteer to catch a profiteer—that sort of thing.

Shaolin took a liking to BD right away. He had never met a large black woman, who wasn't black, before. It was something like making capsules that weren't capsules (oops!!—Ploo let that slip into his notes). So, then, this was WZG's business model, the Shaolin model had wings!!

Shaolin made encapsulated medications to specification, with formulations supplied by the corporation. For 43 trillion capsules, Shaolin needed around 473 trillion gms. of formulation, seeing that each capsule needed 11 gms. of formulation and other stabilizing additives. With a 11 percent wastage or consumption above norms, norm, the consumption of formulation should have been around 525 trillion gms. A truly astonishing statistic, given the fact that (bye the way, Ploo's all time favorite colts at the races were named Astonishing and Squanderer—Squanderer retired to stud undefeated—where he was eventually beaten by a filly who was quite unimpressed and refused his advances—- Astonishing went on to race—and lose—in other countries including the USA) WZG's actual consumption for the past two years was 525 trillion gms. for each year. BD had long since discovered that in most franchise operations, the money in the making was in the wastage norms set by the brand owner. It was amazing (and actually quite foolish) that WZG had consumed precisely the quantity required by the formulation. What was equally amazing:

WZG actually did not have machine hours to produce and package 43 trillion capsules, only the tax deductible wage earning, labor hours (in fact most of WZG's six generations and 11 children showed up as wage earners in the payroll list—some of the dears, being dearly departed and eleven of the dears, being nearly dearly departed).

WZG had one more capsule manufacturing facility, this one in south Mexico. This unit, however, did not receive any formulations from the corporation and turned out FDA capsules, to the tune of 9.428 trillion capsules a year, 8.624 trillion capsules for the previous year, showing a growth of 9.322 percent over the previous year. This was pretty amazing considering that the base was a zero base of no formulation supply.

The capsules processed in the States were FDA approved and branded as Zerantac and the capsules manufactured in south

Mexico were branded as Zeratanc. Zeratanc could not be sold in the States but Zerantac could be sold in south Mexico.

Zerantac was a health stimulant for HIV –ve patients, and Zeratanc was a financial stimulant for WZG. WZG was simply under filling each Zerantac capsule by 11 percent (more additives) and flying the formulation so saved to the unit in south Mexico. The really funny part of it was that some physicians and pharmacists recommended Zertanc as a more potent medication ('buy the one made in south Mexico')—some medics even recommended Zertanc as a more potent drug 'it has something to do with the difference in climate where it is stored and processed'.

The unit in south Mexico never really showed any profits, but WZG and his family (three complete surviving generations and 11 children) had plenty of airfares and hotel stays for research and development to improve the drug. Who knows? WZG may eventually even make the money for the trip to Shaolin!!

Ploo was thrilled. His theory did actually work. People did commit statistically detectable economic fraud. All was (s)well with USA's gdp, Uncle Sam had more under the top hat than he was giving away. CWeathersome was thrilled that his first case was a success—WZG was upset, but then over compensated with a round trip to the Peregrinde Islands (for the informed reader—these islands don't exist—please, please don't waste time googling it—just giggle about it).

Dumpy was realistic—he took up the case of the jewelry shop while the Kid went about filling up the forms at the

University of Bikago—they had to put up a couple of recommendations for the No-bell prize nominations—a leading case was that of a student who had invented a way to
prevent parents from visually seeing their children after the
age of 14 and therefore, was nominated for the Peace Prize,
for promoting world peace. This same student also went
on to win the Miss World contest, also for promoting world
peace—simply amazing what one can achieve at any age,
by promoting world peace—however, an inventor of cheap,
bio degradable, portable public toilets was refused his nomi-
nation for promoting world peace, on the grounds that there
was too much refuse in the model.

The Jewelry shop was owned, managed and staffed by
an Indian (it was becoming difficult to find an 'American' entrepreneur). Ploo complained "Ive seen more white blooded
Americans in Dubai, than Ive seen in the States, Im going to
photograph the next one I see" Ploo declared with an air of
seriousness that was so uncharacteristic of his research profile.
The shop sold jewelry but did not have any jewelry, only books
of jewelry designs. Customers from the local Indian community
ordered jewelry from the books (especially on the occasion
of marriages, births, US festivals, new jobs, graduation, release
from prison, winning cricket match, festivals, home coming,
home leaving, new business, closing business, North Indian
festivals, South Indian festivals—there were even Indian festivals!! imagine!!) and the shop delivered these items within
an agreed time frame (2–3 weeks). This had, simply *had* to
be a straight business, one could not get a simpler, more efficient economic model. This time it was the Kid. Kid Rangy
refused to accept the existence of an authentic business
model, no shadow model. Also, the Kid had a deep dislike for
Indian businessmen—you see, the Kid had his own business!!
(Im not sure what this explained, but as I learnt much later, it
explained a lot—this in the story of Kid's adventures in South
Eastern Virgin Columbia—also doesn't exist as the informed
reader would doubtless have surmised by now).

The Jewelry team was, therefore, the Kid, Dumpy Carthwright (DC), BD, CWeathersome and WZG. WZG's expertise

was considered important because he had some experience with six generations and 11 children, all being illegal immigrants—at least two of them working in law firms and one of them a DA. Three months and 11 weeks later, WZG presented his findings to the EOW. The Indian owning the jewelry shop was Declan Sharma. 'Declan' wasn't an Indian name, but then there wasn't any jewelry in the shop as well, only design books. Ploo wasn't worried about Declan not being an Indian name, "This is the day and age when top golfers are black or Indian (Singh, Chopra etc.) basket ball stars are Chinese, the Pope is German, the earlier Pope was a Pole (once removed—from Poland) and the British are eventually British with the Archbishop of Canterbury doing his own cantering and burying" Ploo sipped his coffee and groaned "Too much mug and too little coffee" he complained.

The prima facie business model was simple—no inventory of jewelry, so no risk of outdated discountable stock, jewelry made to order and style of a specific community, wide range of designs (both western and oriental), reasonable prices (based on oriental price levels), reasonable time frame for delivery and steady demand, in fact growing demand—great income—good income tax payments. Therein was the catch. The demand was growing at a rate faster than the known rate of growth in the presence of the registered Indian community. Ploo looked at WZG "Bhai Hitlers!! There is no Chinese Juice in this one". WZG gave Ploo a funny look "There definitely aren't any Chinese Jews and no thanks to Hitler" his wrinkled face looked even more wrinkled and his white eyebrows looked a bit whiter at the thought of Hitler, Juice and Jews camping in the same sentence (although Hitler himself had never been to Boot Camp—all the more unfortunate—the world could have been saved six years of troubles and birth pangs—there are those who will claim, however, that WWII was engineered ONLY for the SOLE purpose of creating East Germany—it was quite well known by 1926 that East Germany had a lot of masons, who were mainly free, and they had to build a wall—the same thing had happened many many years earlier in China—so they built their wall too—this was

Keynesian economics at its sharpest—Lasker would have been happy).

The catch was that Ploo, WZG, Kid Rangy or CW could not actually conduct any direct enquiries. They had of necessity to approach the whole matter obliquely but then, they discovered to their delight, that Dumpy Carthwright was sufficiently oblique, not just oblique, in fact quite opaque. Ploo settled into his chair (being considered the most experienced EOW), Ploo was expected to come up with the ideas. "Bye Twisters!! Ploo finally exclaimed, "I think I have it—where is the jewelry actually coming in from, for the actual sale? Where are the customers coming in from?—Get me the answers to these questions and we will surely solve our problem!!" Bonaventura Dieasa and Dumpy Carthwright had their doubts. Dumpy (aka Bakuram aka Mouchadkaka to the local populace) switched to a jewelry supplier and asked BD to "pose as a stout, shabbily dressed (not very difficult for BD) potential customer of costumed jewelry".

This little suggestion ended with BD first emptying the contents of a cold cup of coffee over Dumpy's lap and then whacking him on the head with the sole of a stout shoe. Anyway, six months later the investigation was completed. Ploo was relaxing along the pool (the pleasantly contradistincted form of Ploo), looked up and saw Kid Rangy looking pleased with himself "Neta, I mean neat job, Ploo, you really solved it for us, spot on". Ploo looked surprised and then grinned at BD who was standing with Kid and looking every bit a stout, shabbily dressed, customer of costumed jewelry (lots of it). Ploo, however, not wanting a jug of juice over turned on him, wisely refrained from commenting or generously providing his opinion on the so generous proportions of the potential jewelry customer, who had obviously been converted from potential to real customer.

"Bye Goppers, I don't think you really meant that, Rangy (Only Ploo insisted on calling the Kid by his abbreviated family name 'Rangy')" Ploo gestured toward a couple of lounging seats that were lounging in the background. "I don't think I really contributed that much" grimaced Ploo looking for a

spittoon and not finding one and then dramatically swallow-
ing whatever was intended for the spittoon in deference to
Bonaventura Dieasa. Ploo did suffer, as a result an enormous
case of indigestion, however, that story is ---never told. Case
facts as presented by Kid, before the team retired to the buffet (the buffet was so savagely attacked that it was quietly
retired later).

- There was no jewelry in the jewelry shop—never
  was, never had been, never would be—except
  when there were buyers in the shop
- The buyers were the sellers of the jewelry
- The sellers of jewelry were Indians who had traveled
  to the USA, loaded in costumed jewelry that was in
  fact, in most cases their life savings and their ticket
  into the USA (there were settling in and agency
  costs)
- The sellers did not have jewelry to sell, in fact, they
  simply wore the jewelry
- The sellers traveled into the US and walked into the
  jewelry shop and stayed in the US and merged
  with the community

WZG Shaolin recognized the ploy, it was something that
he had used 11 years back, when he had a little problem
of getting hold of 154 dedicated workers for a construction
project (a large commercial building off East Wacker) most
of the construction workers actually continue till this day
to work in the building as janitors, mail delivery personnel,
security guards, office equipment service persons and even
secretaries—this was again taken off from the Middle
East—an entry strategy that a group of Palestinians and
Egyptians had used to great effect in Saudi and Kuwait.

Declan Sharma, the apparent owner of the shop was
an illegal immigrant himself. "Bhai Sharma" Ploo exclaimed
"there just don't seem to be any legal immigrants any more,
anywhere in the world". Declan was also a doctor with a
flourishing practice, paid his taxes, played his golf, watched

his baseball, jogged his jog, ate his hog and paid his muggers—he was well settled in. Declan was a cog, a settled in cog, a leaf on the tree, indistinguishable from the rest. He was also known as Sham Declan and, not quite unsurprisingly had acquired a great deal of knowledge of jewelry and had also acquired a great deal of jewelry. Declan was a dentist and here CW was positively rolling at the case review meeting "Sham really never had a shortage of gold fillings!!" Declan had three children in the States, the eldest of which, at the time was 11 years old and had aspirations to eventually be a Mayor and then a Governor of a major State. One way to become a prominent Mayor was to create a catastrophe (mass water/food poisoning, a stadium crash, a hurricane, raging fires, a bomb threat, a bio bomb threat—were some of the jewelry store owners' ideas) and then to gallantly respond and save the situation with a cool mind—thus developing and election platform of sorts.

"Crumbling Packers" Ploo exclaimed at the end, so surprised that he over turned the jar of juice leaving a sticky, stinky stain on the poolside "At this rate I really don't know what to expect from the rest of the family owned businesses in North America" Kid Rangy grinned "Well at least BD latched on to some of the loot, Dumpy had his teeth done by Declan and WZG Shaolin found an Indian bride" Ploo decided to drop it, the team, his EOW team was behaving like a MEOW team and partaking of the spoils of war, much like Alexander's Generals who took what they saw and let pass what they chose not to see. It is not widely known, but the reason that Alexander lost his battles in India (there were seven) is that his Generals refused to accept that elephants were not large bulls with tusks instead of horns and one just could not use a red flag to an elephant with much success.

There appears little hope for the beleaguered USA until politicians stop referring to the Kingdom of Saudi Arabia as 'Soddy' Arabia (unintentionally highlighting a particular preference in some quarters in the Middle East) and stop referring to the Chinese Yuan as the 'UN'.

India

I ndia is a veritable jugglerknot of economic bundleism. The country has a large manufacturing base and a bludge oning base of services, due to the demographic shift from yoke yielding to mouse wielding youth. Pettiness in social culture is magnified in a dog eat dog, frog jump frog in the pond environment. If an Indian sports association were to hold a hurdles event, the athletes would spend most of the course jumping over each other. India has several sporting world champions (badminton, chess, cricket, shooting, weight lifting, billiards, snooker, to name a few) but no team work. Put a team of Indians together and they are completely internally focused and couldn't beat their grandmother.

The unemployment levels in India are a thing of the past and almost anybody who is willing to accept a job, will find a job. The country is riddled with rich people and is one of the most poverty stricken ruralistic land masses of the mid hemisphere. Indians have a tendency to get their statistics notoriously incorrect, on the side of good color e.g. the President will think that there are 20 m Indians living below the poverty line (August 2007) and there are actually 250 m below a not-to-high poverty line. India's own poverty line is a few metres lower than Lake Superior, comparatively speaking in terms of the definition—who is a poor person? Somebody who eats a decent meal once a week?

On the flip side (here you really have to visualize the pizza man) India is self sufficient in food and largely in engineering and high tech goods as well. India manufactures satellites, is a nuclear weapon state and specializes in missile technology. India supports a resident population of over a billion people and the population continues to grow at the non religioustic rate of around 2 percent annually.

The country's foreign exchange reserves have been steadily growing, in line with the reduction in trade deficits and the overall increase in the volume and quality of exports. The country is still largely a rural land mass, however, the urban elements of society have been drag pulling the rural props into the 21st century.

The country has proven time and again that it is politically stable, after having released itself from the burdens of foreign occupation as recent as a little over 50 years back. This is in stark contrast with its immediate and extremely unfriendly neighbors Pakistan, Bangladesh and Sri Lanka. The Indians and the British parted ways amicably in 1947, the Indians were glad to see the backs of the British, the British were glad to see the backs of Indians, especially Lord Mountbatten, and Indians who chose to do so, went on to live in England, Portugal and France. It is a little known fact that most French cuisine and English sports originated in India—it is so little known, because it is in fact quite untrue.

Consider this, the country is only 58 years old, has a population of over a billion, was plundered for four centuries by the British and yet is a front running economic power. The country's education system, has been continually defined and refined, so that today, the engineering, professional accountancy/auditing, medical, and other streams of education are academically superior to most other countries and aligned with both the country's needs and global needs. Not surprisingly, a significant portion of NASA, IBM, scientists, research personnel and doctors in the USA are persons of Indian origin or are Indian originally (which are two quite different classes). An estimated 30% of top engineering and medical specialists in the USA are of Indian origin, and another 10% are of doubtful Indian origin, with a further 15% of sub prime Indian origin, accounting for a whole 75% of such categories (there is something wrong with the math here, but then the Jews were never good mathematicians).

The challenge before the country is how to bridle growth, so that inflationary pressures do not build up in an overheated, government controlled business environment. Private enterprise and political freedom go hand in hand in this country. And yet the economy needs a larger than life measure of government control to ensure stability. A perennial problem has been that the bureaucrats who run the reserve bank of India—are just that—reserved—and excel in closing the barn door after the bullock has munch the munch.

The transportation system, always an important development index, is well developed, including air, road and sea. However, the rail system is strained from the large population and in several areas, logistics are over crowded out by food and other commodity deliveries, e.g. steel, coal, cement, wheat and other core economic produce. Waterways and coastal sea borne transportation need to be enhanced to facilitate regional commerce in the Indian subcontinent. For far too long the focus has been on roads, rail and air, almost totally and hilariously ignoring transportation across internal and external water ways, that would perhaps be the country's most efficient and cost effective transportation mode.

The country periodically holds 'general' elections with much fanfare and participation. Although it must be said, that 'generals' have studiously avoided the political scene. The country is overly fond of 'melas' the village fair—but on a country wide mega scale. The proliferation of statehood, and the development and release of state boundaries, will convert regional economic glue into dependent states that are not economically viable.

Typically, the Indian economy is dependent upon the monsoon (seasonal rainfall) and the food grain production is only marginally stimulated by planned irrigation, even today. The country probably suffers from one of the highest incidence of corruption leakages of planned developmental government expenditure. India has wholeheartedly dismantled the food management system, the build up of grain reserves and the guarantees of fair price to farmers. This is a critical country risk and the economy now is always only one monsoon away from total disaster. Grain stocks are perilously low as the country single mindedly pursues economic industrial development and focuses on managing its oil imports bill. Farmers are hit in good times (low prices) and bad times (no crops) and farmer suicides is an increasing trend over the past few years.

The consistent felling of environmental protection is systemic and has been a major cause and source of poverty, especially in the rural and semi urban areas. The Indian tiger is now literally and euphemistically a true paper tiger. The ever fertile Chinese keep thinking that shark fins and tiger bones will enable them to increase their population man fold (quite possible in advance preparation of an invasion into Australia). The Indian business environment is characterized by poor management skills and even poorer planning and capacity build up. The average Indian industrialist is on a self destruct mode, even while at the peak of his build up through accumulation of tax evasive and evaded wealth. Indian business houses rarely, if ever, think quality (on a global standard scale) and economic size. The general tendency is to minimize both quality and scale of operations until the entrepreneur can effectively monitor and count cash take home on a daily basis. The economy is largely cash, land, gold jewelry linked (necessarily in that destructive order of financial illiquidity—these are extremely illiquid current assets), has been that way for roughly 7.5 thousand years (earliest known record of monkey kings—at latest reports, monkeys have begun to re rule the capital city with at least one city official being unceremoniously dethroned from his balcony). Most economic and demographic historians have shown a marked inability to work behind the 5,000 year curtain—this is unfortunate, then again, maybe not—much like looking behind a mirror.

The lifestyle of the urbanesque Indian has shown change beyond compare during the past ten years. Indians are now moving from a positive state of wallowing in abject poverty to the more mundane aspects of conspicuous consumption and wanton waste. This is not necessarily a good thing but it is change and a shift of focus from the green, grass growing highly overrated food revolution to focus on the services sector. It still will not halt farmer suicides and the drowning of cash crops in a bath of corrupting and land destructive fertilizers.

Never mind the imbalances in development and the vast numbers below the poverty line. These are but natural characteristics of a populous nation and within the next 25 years or so, India will have fewer villages, more towns and more cities, with at least one more metro. Currently, India has only one metro—Mumbai, that is also the commercial capital. It is a sad commentary that India has a commercial capital, an industrial capital, a political capital but little intellectual capital. The Bongalis who used to provide the intellectual and cultural capital in the past, are now obsessed it seems with the lack of quality fish in the markets and quality politicians in the legislature—which comes first for a Bongali—the fish or the politician? This is a chicken and yokeless egg question from the days the Bongali welcomed the East Indian

Company with open arms and baskets of fish. Hardly surprising that some of the most ardent independence movement pillars are Bongalis—these were the same guys who actually gave it away by the baskets in the 1600's.

There is a lot for the Westerner to complain about. Although why the Westerner should complain about India's problems is beyond the scope of fiction. This is much like the Westerner complaining about the problems of the Islamic world. Point noted is that the Westerner rarely complains about his own problems, unless it is to say that Chinese firms have poisoned his toys. Needless, at this population level there is a lot anybody will complain about, anywhere, in any country, any society. Further, take into account the fact that the country is only 58 or so years old and has been veritably looted for over four hundred years and a lot of what you see sort of falls into place. Amazing turnaround story and a good one for the West to follow. I suspect that by 2030, the West will follow the Indian model. The Indian model was based on a few essentials:

- Government enterprise
- Government subsidies
- Expansion and support of the rail network
- Support for the small/small scale entrepreneur
- Covert support for the few large entrepreneurs through tailored fiscal policies
- Focus on and support for the farmer, at least for two decades (1960s through to early 1980s)
- An open policy toward new technologies, such as the information technology sector
- No ridiculous government funded health care and pension schemes (scams?)
- Government expenditure on primary and higher education; and
- Focus and support for export oriented industries.

A quick look at the list above will show that the West and the USA in particular have moved far away from the basics. The resultant is huge trade deficits, a tottering currency and an impoverished and unsupported farm sector. No country can get very far, for very long, without the basics and the Indian, Chinese and South Korean economies have stuck hard to the basics for over 50 years now. The big Indian rope trick risk is now the abandonment of the farmer. Farmers in India are generally a famished, unsupported lot.

Government subsidies rule and free trade is often quite disastrous. This is simply because if a country does not support its own producers and manufacturers, nobody else will and that will lead to political and social instability. Subsidies rule, expenditure on defense, star wars and space exploration are damaging to the economy. The Indian and sub continent economies, in general, have been hurt in part by the USA fuelled poor security environment, as in the Middle East, with military adventurism actively encouraged and morphed democratic regimes, backed by military power, supported to damage the economic fabric that threatens the West. The USA has in the past (and continues) exported economic, political and social insecurity and instability. This is perhaps the core role of a world power, the same with the Romans, the British, the USSR and now the USA. World powers use their capital resources to develop dependency relationships with countries by weakening their economic and social fabric—this is what the USA is still attempting in SE Asia and in the ME.

India needs to support the farmer, for nearly 25 years now, all the support has been directed at industry and services. India needs to have better land management laws, better laws for exploitation of natural resources (better late than never).

The three dimensional resource utilization plan needs to be implemented immediately. The country needs to focus on land, sea and air resources and reserves. Water way rights, water way mineral reserves and air rights are valuable but completely neglected resources in India.

India needs a presidential system of democracy—this is perhaps the only idea that India can borrow from the USA. India should couple that with the concept of a royal family (borrowed from Europe, originally borrowed from India) and perhaps the Gandhi family lends itself to form the core of a royal family system. Princes are in, industrialists are out, the need of the hour is to support the humble farmer and send the fumble harmers packing. Also India in the full spirit of boundary recognition should release Goa to the Portugese (i.e. re liberate Goa from India) and Kashmir to the kashmiri nationals (not Pakistan). Nepal should be part of India, it has its own royal family, or rather, what's sadly left of it. A little distancing from Sri Lanka's problems would help regional peace. Pakistan will eventually go the Afghanistan way—again the principle of comparative advantage. Some countries supply security, some countries supply poppy and some supply terror. Demand of course always exists, everywhere, every time, for whatever we don't have, we want. Politically a large measure of stability could be achieved by introducing a proper presidential form of democracy and a formalized and regulated system of royal families (Europe is a shining example). The Queens of Europe are always late.

Kuwait

Kuwait is an oil reserve, as distinguished from 'Kuwait has oil reserves'. Kuwait is essentially a largish oil field. The country has anywhere between 5 percent to 12 percent of the world's known oil reserves, depending on whether the drilling is on shore, off shore, vertical or horizontal or just plain imaginary.

So what ails Kuwait, if at all anything? Kuwait has an abundance of a single resource and unfortunately a relatively small population of around a million Kuwaiti nationals. To be economically sustainable in the long run, the country needs a population of at least around 7 million nationals. At this level, Kuwait would be economically stable and secure, in equilibrium. Beyond this level, Kuwait will find it difficult to manage the demands on land and the demands of growing unemployment. Countries such as India, find themselves in a perpetual state of economic disequilibrium since they have crossed the economic land mass supportable population size, whereas, Australia for example is under populatized (human resource intellectual capital per measure of land mass).

At the current level of population, Kuwait has an alarming estimated 30,000 plus unemployed Kuwaitis, around 150,000 under employed Kuwaitis and around 15,000 unemployed expatriates. This disturbing state of affairs is principally due to:

■　　　Improper investment policies that channel oil revenues into Western economies or other GCC countries) with little Kuwaiti economic benefit, and with a range of possible and actual investment speculation losses. Kuwait's industrial sector is poorly developed. Kuwaiti businessmen prefer to open stores for high street fashion clothing rather than build value through industry.

■　　　Funding of the effort of war on various Middle East countries. This is wasteful expenditure that Kuwait cannot really afford. Once again little or no benefit to the local population. Kuwait should join other Arab nations in requesting, most politely, the regime of the USA to leave the Middle East alone. It is clear that instead of a peace process, the USA has supported a 'pieces' process. We wont say 'USA and allies' since Tony Blair does not really constitute an ally, as distinguished from a pet.

■　　　Too much focus on the oil sector and not enough investment in infrastructure. Many roads are in terrible shape, water ways for commuting have not been developed and Kuwait's beautiful islands have not been developed—for insecurity reasons—as distinguished from security reasons.

- Inadequate investment in the education sector and therefore, many Kuwaitis are unable to acquire in Kuwait. the skills and academic qualifications required by the business environment—a typical resource development mismatch - .

- Alignment of the currency with the dollar. This is a disastrous monetary and political policy. Oil exports should be denominated in Euros and in part should be commodity exchange denominated, like the old USSR regime agreements with its allies.

- Inadequate attention in healthcare. The health-care system is in terrible shape and most who can afford it would do a simple dental treatment over-seas. Good doctors are reluctant to work in Kuwait. Most expatriate doctors are from nearby Lebanon and Egypt, with inadequate experience in working with cutting edge (sic/sick pun) technology. There is also a huge need for proper diabetic, cardiac, nephorology and special needs care units.

- Focus on importing cheap labor from South Asian (India, Bangladesh, Sri Lanka, Phillipines, Pakistan) countries, instead of injecting quality human re-sources who could train local resources. The qual-ity of resources is overwhelming labor class with little quality or efficiency to contribute. The major-ity of third country visas issued are for cooks, driv-ers, cleaners. And the majority of them have to learn cooking, driving and cleaning after their ar-rival in Kuwait. This abysmally low quality of human resource imports in fact places a huge strain on the infrastructure, simply because the value add per person is extremely low. The index of expatri-ate value add (IEVA) for Kuwait is lower than only for Canada and France. Kuwait should shift focus to importing human resources from South Africa, France, Poland, Romania, Armenia and languish-ing EU countries. Kuwait has probably the highest per capita maids, drivers, cooks and cleaners in the world. At supermarkets it is quite common to see a national have three South Asians take his shopping cart to his four wheel drive (in which at least one, maybe two, maids watch the children).

The security environment has been superbly managed by the ruling family and as a result Kuwait has and will continue to enjoy a large degree of political and economic stability until around 2015. Long term, smaller countries such as Kuwait will face serious security threats (by around 2030), since both Saudi Arabia and Iraq covet Kuwait's resource rich territory, just as Iran covets Bahrain. In the Indian sub continent, Nepal and Bangladesh are not long term sustainable countries and there is a view that by 2015, Pakistan will also disintegrate under the sheer weight of the un governed north eastern frontiers. Nepal will most likely, be quietly absorbed by China who at latest reports are already building a highway through the mountains—all their highways have a military objective—these are unlike the Keynesian Great Wall of China.

Kuwait has aggressively disturbed the regional political balance by whole heartedly supporting the propaganda machine of twisted 'global' democracies with ill willed military adventurism. All the extremely good work carried out by Ronald Reagan, Pope John Paul II, Gorbachov, George Bush (Sr.) and Bill Clinton, has been almost entirely undone by George Bush (Jr.) and Tony Blair. The latter two being fierce opponents of world peace and quite literally the devils' advocates. The Axis of Evil is as true as the Axis of D-evil, and D came before E. The Iranian, Iraqi, Korean, Pakistani, Kurdish and Lebanese troubles were entirely manufactured by this duo of evil. Terrorism was corporatized by this duo, and made a household buzzword. A fundamental economic principle religiously followed by this duo of evil, was that war is the engine of economic growth. The definitions of democracy, liberation, terror, insurgents, nationalism are now all confused in the Middle East. This confusion has already contaminated the democracies of the West. The liberators are really the conquering invaders and the saved are the vanquished victims. The traditional definition of defense spending has now been twisted to 'attack' spending.

The country has huge potential and with the current limited population, it is actually easy to correct the imbalances and carry out a structural surgery. To do that economic and political policies should undergo significant change.

Kuwait should for example develop its national carrier (airline) and take the lead in the commercial development of alternative fuel sources and establish a base for research in the pharmaceutical industry, considering its proximity to Asian and other populous countries, for ease of clinical trials and numbers. Water ways transportation should be developed by Kuwait throughout the region. Port cities always have infinitely more value and less security related issues than airports and metros. Economists and finance ministers have short memories and what most of them forget is that economic growth for thousands of years has been fuelled by water way/sea/ocean transport rather than by airports. An A 380 looks pretty (there are divergent views on this) but a ship is a ship is a ship—for sheer economy, anti polluting, bulk carrying and speed (yes, speed—regionally it is quicker to transport through well developed water ways).

Kuwait should also forge deep relationships with neighboring countries and immediately float a stable currency. Large investments by the Government are required in the education sector. Government intervention helps, particularly where private enterprise will hold the view that returns are not quick and that deep reserves are required to fund the gestation period. In a growing economy, private investments will always target quick trading type returns through the stock exchanges rather than green field projects.

The proper harnessing of natural reserves and the development of relationships with other neighboring countries are perhaps key, even more important than developing alternative sources of gross domestic product.

It is important for Kuwait to think long term, beyond the wastage and depletion of the natural resource. To advance the cause of Kuwait as a land connectivity and research

base. This is of course possible if Government funding for infrastructure projects takes off. Further, the economy should shift from a predominantly export oriented economic model to a model where resources and natural reserves are consumed internally, to produce value added products that are exported.

Over 90% of the upstream production should be processed internally and that is the key to the long term survival of this economy. The development of alternate fuel sources/ concepts is perhaps less important than building deep regional relationships with it neighbors. The interactional trade and support services is important from a long term perspective. The economy currently is isolated socially, culturally and politically. This degree of isolation (8 on the rating scale for developing economies) harbors no good and it is essential for stability to have an interactive economy, regionally and locally.

Produce, process, trade, interact—these are the keys that will facilitate a quick turnaround for the Kuwaiti economy, this is what will enable it to sustain a dynamic, quality human resource level of around 7 million on a long term basis (the country does not have land mass or actual or notional resources to support more than 7 million people within the framework of a developing economy).

Kuwait will therefore, take another fifty years of careful management of economic resources, to break the mould and spread its wings. Careful handling of the regional political situation is critical to economic stability. The oil resources, in effect slow down the developmental process, since they push the country into the upstream—export mode, instead of the trade, interact, value-add mode.

The ruling family has been a benevolent guiding hand and this has significantly helped the Kuwaiti national to an appreciable level of prosperity. This is not a country for governing by pacemakers, rather governing by pace setters of the younger generation. Recent capital market restrictions are regressive in nature. Further, for some reason, the country has not implemented an effective progressive taxation system based on ability to pay—this has to a large extent resulted in the unfortunate neglect of infrastructure development. Kuwait, however, is the strategic pulpit and balcony of the Middle East.

The Problem of France

This is not actually only about France. It is about all European and North American countries (including the UK, since classified by Tony Blair as an NA country), that take in large numbers of immigrants. The classic policy mistake has been to provide at some stage nationality to immigrants. What these countries should do is provide work permits and entry rights only to those who have secured employment. Employment can be regulated through issue of limited number of work permits to registered agents/cies. The right to stay and live in these adopted countries for immigrants should be directly linked to the right to work and contribute to the economy.

Immigration should not result in a burden on the health care, sanitation, security and education systems. Immigrants should not be entitled to free health care and education for themselves, or children or parents. Similarly, immigrants should not be provided with property ownership rights and should be subjected to income taxes. Employers of immigrants should pay their governments a cess that will support employment and wage levels of nationals. The immigrant population typically places a huge burden on the infrastructure—transportation, electricity, water are all scarce and costly resources. In several cases immigrant populations are possibly responsible for

insurgency threats, cultural and social upheaval, high crime rates and football hooliganism.

Australia

Australia is a continent with five major cities, namely, Perth, Melbourne, Sydney, Brisbane and Adelaide, the others don't really count. Australia is also a racist country like the USA and has for long driven the aborigines from their lands. Adelaide is so distant from the others, so as almost to be in another country. Australia is a large continent with the mineral ore base forming the basis for the mining industry economy and the large farm land providing the grazing necessary to run large herds of the four legged variety. The local populace of Australia and New Zealand are of criminal origin and largely racist and myopic. There is, however, some hope that the Australians will vote out Howardian gimmickry. Poor Howard never really understood global politics and was essentially a fumble harmer.

The country has developed copper mines rather cost effectively. The risks are of course huge with such an economic model. The mining industry is characterized by fluctuations in the metal price, rendering some mines immediately economically disastrical in a theatrical sort of way since whole towns may come to depend upon a small cluster of marginally exploitable mining rights. These mining towns are also called

Australia's One Hole towns—one Church, supermarket, pub, hotel, school, drug store, gym etc.

The country has well established, simple and effective legal, taxation and transportation systems, although the airline sector is rather out of focus. The airline sector trapezes regularly between long haul and short haul hub and spoke operations, with cargo operations being the neglected step child. Most aircraft in Australia should be combis to ensure effective utilization over the continent.

Australia has a wonderful people (forgetting for a moment the racism, criminalization and fondness for alcohol), a wonderful human resource development policy. The first things that strike you are that this economic model has a few large minuses and therefore instability:

- Population of this country is only around 25 million. This is simply unsustainable for a land mass of this size. Long term basis projective estimates show that a sustainable population for Australia is more like 125 million to 150 million. Water resources can be obviously developed through desalination plants—again a neglected opportunity.
- The land mass is currently grossly underutilized and over mined. Australia needs to ensure equitable exploitation of the available land mass to over 50% from the current 4%. Most of central Australia is a wilderness that harbors mainly spiders.
- Australia needs at least twelve large cities as compared with the current five. Townsville, Hobart, and the like don't really count. Even Perth would not qualify as a city by Asian size standards and Brisbane stutters perennially on the brink of the definition. Sydney and Melbourne are cities, although at last count, Melbourne seems to be shrinking—clearly a case of Mistaken Bourne Identity.
- Overdependence on only two major sources of gross (in a decent sort of way, here) domestic product.

■   Non value addition to the base resource (similar problem afflicts Kuwait!!). A pattern emerges. Where there is a resource abundance, value addition does not necessarily happen or is not necessarily planned, simply because economic wealth is

to be had easily. Economically speaking, resource rich countries are generally poorly equipped to handle the impact of business cycles and also do not manage overall success in growth (since it occurs too easily in the first place).

■   Agriculturally archaic practices. This is likely to be the single most limiting factor for the economic development of this country, together with abysmally low levels of education among the local population. For long, Australians have sincerely believed that they could import cheap labor (from China) and cheap brains (from India) — a logical conclusion from that is that if both these inputs are imported, then all the Australian provides is farm feed and criminalization. Agricultural production needs to be significantly enhanced, possibly over ten times over current levels. This is of course possible only with the effective integration of the aboriginal population and the utilization of the central land mass. Mass irrigation through desalination plants at coastal areas is the key to this particular development issue.

Australia remains agriculturally under developed and this seems to be a huge economic weakness and dependency.

■ Port development. The ports need to be developed to facilitate exports of value add products. Australia needs to significantly increase the volume and value of value add processes and products through the port facilities, especially in the North, toward connecting routes through Asia.

Geographically, Australia is temporarily isolated, until the land mass joins up with Asia major (this is inevitable). This is a major drawback and this isolationism will eventually lead to economically virulent in breeding. The isolated nature of the economy will encourage large scale business environment in—breeding and this will genetically create defective and weak business mechanisms and democratic institutions. For example, the Australian political system has long been characterized by a ridiculous polarization and overly simplified system of the Labor and the Not so Labor parties—the age old blak and vite controversy.

Australia needs to guard against this economic isolationism and economic in breeding. One solution is to use large, albeit more expensive transport alternatives, cutting the transport time, through air. The increase in cost of transportation could be offset by the benefits of the wholesome development of the inner and middle land mass. The requirement for development could fuel a market of its own making, creating a need for Australian value add products that are processed and delivered efficiently and cost effectively. Australia could benefit hugely with a policy to encourage immigration from African nations, instead of encouraging illegal immigration from China. The current policy seems destined to convert Australia into China's new Hong Kong—socially and economically.

The Australian dollar should be converted to the Australian Quaterbak. This will ensure that the traded value of the currency will be relatively stable. The current weakness of the currency will dissipate within a short time as a result of the increase in population and utilization index of the available land mass. The steady and progressive taxation policies have resulted in a significant amount of interest in foreign investment, however, there is scope for improvement.

The biggest danger that Australia faces is the threat of economic isolation and a slow growing population. The small increase in population and low density will create demand bottlenecks and halt economic progress. Australia needs to dynamically grow the population and increase the land mass utilization, through progressive immigration policies and attractively structure health care and retirement benefits schemes. Australia has the potential to grow far beyond and faster than say, for example, North America and the lower Mediterranean. The development of the agricultural sector through measures such as irrigation through desalination could produce Asiatic economic growth rates. Finally, a word on sport—Australia boasts of the one alien cricketer—the Don. The Don hails from a group of select few alien sportsmen—Bjorn Borg, Jesse Owens and Emmanuel Lasker (being the other three)—who were altogether around a 100 years ahead of their time. Other aliens in other fields, similarly revolutionized scientific and industrial development. There is some controversy about whether Carl Lewis was also an alien—this matter has not been put to rest—especially after the claims of Michael Jackson, Mohammed Ali and Elvis Prestley fans about their alienism. Gandhi from India was an alien, but then he was an alien in every sense even in his own country and was finally put down for that—so it is altogether inconclusive as to whether Gandhi was an alien.

Theory and Practice of Displaced Economics

The 10 Blunders of the World
The Tablet (Medicated) of 10 Commandments of Economics

1. Cash economies:

For years various countries have attempted measures to control and even limit the cash (black, non tax paying) economy. This is quite illogical. The cash economy is an essential economic driving engine and an inevitable fact. This should be recognized as such. It is not necessarily an undesirable element of the economy and in fact central banks should have a cashonomic policy that could in some circumstances be as useful as fiscal policy to curb inflation, manage currency values or to spur growth. Tax evasion has considerable potential upside economic effects. In fact a substantial, almost 30% of the growth in S Korea, Russia, India, Brazil and China (KRIBC) is through the non tax - cash paying economy. Some sectors are designated as non tax paying (e.g. agricultural income in some countries), whereas, several sectors are especially prone to tax evasion and accumulation of unaccounted (non tax paying) wealth and assets. In a private economy this is a major incentive to privatization and entrepreneurship. Neglect of this sector is the first economic blunder (as opposed to wonder) of the world. Taxes not paid and ill gotten illegal gains are economic savings that facilitate economic development. Such gains are typically ploughed back into the economy with amazing speed unlike legitimate 'declared' gains that are filed with the authorities. Another feature is that if the tax regime (the only worthwhile true regime change required in the 21st centuries) is changed to an expenditure basis, instead of the usual income basis, the cash economy will no longer be considered an evil, gross aspect of gross domestic product.

2. Bankruptcy Code:

The one sparkling feature in the USA economy is the relatively lax bankruptcy code. This has been a great incentive to entrepreneurship. BRICK (Brazil, Russia, India, China, Korea) countries would do well to emulate this example and provoke private enterprise through an accommodating bankruptcy code. This is truly the second blunder of the world, that is, not having a proper bankruptcy code, uniform across countries. This is the one aspect of commercial legislation that the USA has got one hundred percent right—in principle, not in application.

3. Subsidies:

Subsidies and tariffs should be implemented vigorously by governments. This will protect indigenous enterprise, provide government revenues and re allocate foreign exchange reserves to priority sectors. Reduction of subsidies is the third blunder of the world. Governments should be slow and careful to encourage imports and disturb the internal balances of inefficient production and the spirit of un competitive disadvantages.

4. Foreign exchange control:

As BRICK economies gain larger foreign exchange reserves, the tendency is to avoid forex management. This is a Himalayan blunder. Forex reserves are not economic reserves, they are in fact strategic reserves that may be leveraged for economic development and for security purposes. Forex management should be de linked from economic goals and carefully marshaled forex reserves can be used to provide insulation from expansionary goals of 'global' powers. This is the fourth blunder of the world. The old USSR practice of managing the rouble through exchange-barter type agreements can be employed with huge benefits especially for imports of energy resources (read crude oil and gas) and defense systems (read F-16, Mirage and Sukhoi).

5. Education, housing and health care:

An economy is in the long term only as good as its education, housing and health care reforms and structure. These are basic pillars of a country. Unfortunately most countries have defense budgets that are significantly higher than housing and health care budgets. Neglect of this sector is the fifth blunder of the world. Expenditure in this area should be always classified as capital expenditure, not as revenue expenditure. Education budgets should receive far greater priority than they currently do in the developed world. The developed world is also characterized by a total inadequacy of health care systems and a gradual but steady increase in the numbers of homeless. Now, the number of homeless people in the USA is huge and far exceeds the number of such homeless peoples in many many countries—note that there is a huge difference between homeless people and pavement dwellers, you may live in a house and yet be quite homeless. A significant proportion of homeless and houseless persons in the USA are those who have served at some time in the military in various capacities, although at latest count, there were no Generals in such a situation. The Middle East also houses a large number of homeless expatriates, who still are unable to afford homes, back home, and spend on houses that do not belong to them, in the country where they are employed.

6. Rationing:

Economies have shifted away from the government policy of building strategic energy and food reserves. This has led to an almost complete dismantling of the rationing system for key commodities. This is the sixth blunder of the world. The economically disadvantaged should be provided both sale and purchase price support. The producer should be compensated for his efforts based on a WACC (applies even for the farm sector) and consumers should be able to purchase at the minimum essential levels of strategic resources. This is the only policy that will ensure longer term social stability. Much of the social unrest in countries such as France, Italy and the Philipines is due to the neglect of this policy. Subsidies and rationing are the same side of two coins. This is a three sided coin, if one takes into account tariffs and power subsidies. There is nothing wrong and everything right with rationing and price support systems to provide the needy with necessities.

7. Pensions:

This is the seventh economic Himalayan blunder of the world. Most countries have attempted to use their economic gains to provide retirement benefits, also known variously as comfort pensions to their ageing populations. Firstly, such a policy is an undesirable economic burden (it actually encourages people to retire and grow old and un productive—in a reckless sort of way, always assuming along the way that the government will take care of them after a particular age). It discourages people from using their productive years to save money and places a huge disincentive on youth. Intra country pensions are therefore not recommended. Instead youth should be provided with incentive (even negative inducement) to save for their retirement years through savings instruments of their own choice. However, the sole exception to this could be related economies. For example if two economies are related, the youth of one country could pay a tax for the ageing population of another. This would encourage savings as well as nurturing experienced human resources. For example the large youthful populations in India, China, Middle Eastern countries could pay a futures tax to support the ageing population in European countries (such as France, Spain, Portugal, Italy, Germany). In return these provider countries could reduce defense and nuclear technology spending leveraging existing assets in Europe. At latest estimates, given the current rate of savings and population growth, it would take the USA 487 years to fully repay its external debt, even without taking into account interest payments—however, it is unlikely that the USA will be actually called upon to repay its entire external debt—this is on the basis of the going concern assumption.

8. Taxation:

Taxation policies are widely messed up across the globe. Taxation is viewed and managed as government revenues and this is the eight Himalayan blunder of the world. Taxes are not governmental revenues. Taxes are not the plunder of elections to be distributed by corrupt politicians among their corrupt constituents. Taxes are resource reallocation incentives and governments should provide full transparency for utilization of tax revenues. Taxes are not sources for governments to cover their non plan revenue expenses (i.e. governmental departmental or governmental bodies/corporation revenue budgets). Governmental bodies should recover revenues based on an activity based expenditure analysis that should result in a cess on user groups. This is a focused way of trimming governmental expenditure and reducing the pinch on the common man. The two largest wasteful uses of scarce economic resources in any country are governmental expenditure and defense expenditure in that order. This holds good for all countries. Taxes and cess should be zero based. Most countries create tax pools that are enlargened each year (using the commonly applied, and totally illogical previous percentage basis method) to provide for higher governmental revenues. In fact there is a school of thought that governmental revenues should be provided for only through printing money. Thus governmental expenditure will be controlled since there will be a direct relation between such expenditure and inflation.

9. Intellectual property rights:

The demand for protection of intellectual property rights, music rights, film/movie rights, copyrights and patents is the ninth Himalayan blunder of the world. These are not assets and therefore are not rights in a free world. Government policy artificially creates such rights and stunts economic development. The abolition of intellectual property rights, copyrights and patents would give tremendous boost to innovation and private enterprise as well as reduce significantly the costs of production and distribution. IPR is a distasteful practice designed by developed nations to cement their economic grip over poor African nations. It is painfully obvious that the poorest of the poor, pay the highest for the 'IPRs' of developed countries. In effect the IPR system is used by developed countries and their large corporations to pass on the research and development expenditures to a host of developing, technology hungry nations. These developing nations actually are paying for the expensive, inefficient and often grossly corrupt research enterprises of the West.

10. Inflation:

Inflation is usually seen as an evil, by most economists and by the common man too (rarely do common woman pay much attention to the subject—seeing that is the man who coughs up in 90% of families). This is the tenth Himalayan blunder of the world. Inflation is parasitical in nature. Inflation needs a host and a cost base. Inflation can live provided it does not kill the host. Inflation is a measure and driver of economic stimulus. Central banks mistakenly track and attempt to limit inflation artificially. This is a bit like having a dog and doing the barking on his behalf or a bit like the tail wagging the dog or a bit like killing the dog to kill the ticks, or a bit like expecting my Iranian Pesian cat to live with a dog as a housemate. Economic growth is at least partly fueled by inflation and cash economics. In the real world (as opposed to economic research labs) around 30% of nominal gdp growth is fueled by cash economics and another 20% real gdp growth is fueled by inflationary forces. Inflation of anywhere up to 15% is just great and absolutely recommended. Red flags to be issued when inflation crosses 10%. Inflation above 10% should be monitored and cooled by demonetization and lowering of wages. Rarely do policy makers see lowering of wages as an effective measure to combat inflation.

In principle and in practice, one just cannot buy when the pocket is empty—the principle of *'nothing chases nothing'*. The inflation index should be computed only with reference to retail prices in metros or at least 60% weighted towards this. India for example, proudly states that its inflation is below 8%, however, this is calculated with reference to rural products and completely ignores spiraling real estate costs and retail prices in metros. The salaried employee in such situations is particularly hard hit since salary incomes lag behind by around 40% of inflation in metros, while tax and insurance costs keep climbing. Typically, in India and China, inflation in metro cities rages at around 30% (much like the West Coast wild fires). This of course cannot be reported by the powers that be—so inflation indices are based on food products of the rural poor. An inflation index based on such rural food products rarely rises, simply because the inflation-ary pressures are not there—the application of the principle 'nothing chases nothing'—a lack of increasing liquidity and little money in the hands of the rural people causes prices to rise slowly—you can't charge something that people can't pay.

The 5th Gear

Political Processes:

A major failure of developed nations is the almost complete failure of political processes. Democracy is almost universally a failed notion. Numerous versions of democracy exist today. India is an illiterate democracy and neighbor Pakistan is a military democracy (both in India and Pakistan, bogus voting abounds and votes can be purchased for as little as Rs.20 (equivalent roughly to half a dollar), the State of Kuwait is a ruling family democracy and so on. The USA has its own version of democracy with managed voting and managed vote counts. The UK has established hereditary democracy with Tony Blair handing over the reins to Gordon Brown. And Iraq of course has established a sort of violent cow-body-countish democracy. Afghanistan has a waiter-ish illegitimate democracy supported by the USA and NATO, that longs internally, like a birth long delayed to return to a more traditional form of government—the NATO and the USA actually have no business being in Afghanistan—there are no WMDs, no nuclear program, no nothing, not even oil—but then, that is another quiet legacy of Colin Powell who fought hard to get the USA into Afghanistan with no back door.

Political parties should be corporatized and listed on stock exchanges. That will allow them access to capital (politicians in the USA would, therefore, not have to worry about funding from China or Israel or for that matters from biased lobbyists in the USA itself—e.g. Hillary Clinton and others may support the military governor of Pakistan because of election funding receipts from his lobbyists). People should be allowed a share in the corporate coffer and elections can even be eventually abolished. One merely has to track stock price on specific stock exchanges. This would also avoid the immense cost and effort involved in elections that are usually stage managed in the most controlled environments. 'Free and fair' elections are few and far between. Elections have never been free nor fair, not since the Roman times.

Defense/Attack Expenditure:

This is a political cost, not a defense cost. A country with the proper political climate will not need to expend large amounts on external defense. Defense expenditure is waste-ful and destructive in more ways than one. For example cost control is usually poor and defense budgets and programs allow typically for as much as 45% non value adding waste. Poor political management increases defense expenditure. Politicians either create an insecure environment by their pol-icies or else foster an apparition of insecurity, so as to allow for permanency in their seats of power. Further, most countries have a defense budget and an in built 'attack' budget. For example only a fraction of the USA' defense budget is defense related, the vast majority of it being attack related, especially with regard to the export of currency and social instability. A typical example of wasteful expenditure on weapons is the Palestine—Jewish (incorrect here to use the word Israeli) conflict, where weapons are used indiscriminately on innocent Palestinians with little hope of any sort of improvement in the situation—but then the occupiers are rarely concerned with improvements in the security situation.

Education (the dilemma of 'post-its'):

Higher education usually lends itself to little control. Typically most countries would benefit from less higher education (leads to little hire) and more technical, vocational training (nursing, teaching, basic engineering, hospitality/catering, fire/safety/security, real estate management etc. Courses and training that is job (hire) oriented instead of courses that are paper degree oriented. A large number of 'post' graduates, for example, in India work finally in manual labor classified jobs, some of them literally in the postal services (it is not unusual to find post graduates driving public transport in the metros—in the capital city, monkeys have it better). The term graduate is perhaps one of the most misused words globally. Less than 2% of those with a high school education are actually fit for further academic pursuit. Many other pursue 'higher' education for want of anything better to do in those formative years—it usually translates into a 4–5 year time killer. All of these would be better served by learning useful career oriented skills that offer hire prospects. This especially important in view of the fact that keeping up employment numbers is one of the keys to economic development—value added by the human resource population would be much higher. How many secretaries, drivers, cooks, maids, fruit pickers, gas station attendants, hair stylists, graphic designers, fashion designers, media specialists, journalists, bank and other financial functionaries, insurance functionaries and Macjobs does a country need? How many doctors, doctorates, post graduates, management graduates, and graduates (aka 'post-its) does a country need? The answers are ridiculously simple—more Macjobs than currently available and less post-its than currently available. Are post-its supported by government subsidies or by soft loan programs (once again the costs are passed on elsewhere). How many post-it jobs are actually rendered obsolete with gains through computerization each year? How many skilled engineers work as electricians and maintenance workers in Canada, how many trained oil sector workers work as drivers in Venezuela, how many doctors work as parking lot attendants in Canada?

Infrastructure:

Infrastructure has long been the domain of governments across the globe. Why? Not in fact because private sector has shied away, not because amounts of investments are huge and payback periods are long. Traditionally governments have held onto infrastructure projects (certainly not because governments build bridges the best), only simply because infrastructure (ports, airports, bridges, dams, irrigation, power etc.) projects offer the single largest-minimum effort opportunity for corruption and for skimming the milk, creaming the cream. In addition to projects that exist on paper, cost build ups, project cost overruns, liberal contractor payments, savings on poor material content etc. a key factor that spin off infrastructure projects lend themselves greatly to 'requests' for 'speed' money. This is to assure the entrepreneur that such projects/approvals for related projects will be granted expeditiously and will not hit unseen hurdles. Infrastructure should be completely privatized and if government invested, should be funded entirely from printed money that should be publicly reported each month by the government, aggregated at a national level. It is a well established fact that any country would spend less on infrastructure if it was privatized, not because of a reduction in absolute effort, but because of a drastic reduction in corruption.

Privatization:

The privatization of traditional governmental instruments and bodies is critical. For example prison systems, law and order and the judicial systems should be privatized with only marginal supervision from elected governmental representatives. There is absolutely no reason why governments or dictators should run the prisons and the judiciary. Governments should merely set the policy and the rules. People accessing the systems and benefiting from the systems should pay for the services. Prisons and judiciary are not like public libraries or museums. Cost efficiency and effectiveness can be achieved only with privatization of fundamental judiciary and security institutions. The postal systems and air carriers are other examples of disastrous government intervention. Governmental intervention in financial systems e.g. nationalization of banks, has led to huge inefficiencies and poor service. Some key sectors that would be better off with privatization, in all countries include:

1. Postal systems
2. Judicial systems including prison systems, law and order
3. Air carriers, there is no need for the ridiculous concept of 'national' carrier—the only true 'national carrier' is ultimately the poor taxpayer
4. Port management—air and sea
5. Highway construction and management
6. Power generation, distribution and management
7. Telephone systems, construction and distribution of resources
8. Heavy industries—refineries and other capital intensive industries
9. Mining and development
10. Energy systems, construction, development and distribution

Essentially, governments can hardly be expected to constitute a political system and run businesses. The core competency of governments is politics, not managing business or currency. The brilliant reformist Indian prime minister—PV N Rao recognized this basic fact and appointed professionals to manage and turnaround the economy, with great success, at the time when the Indian economy had to pledge gold with the BoE. Needless, to say, PVNR was one of the few post independent prime ministers in developing economies to complete a full five year term, before the 'social' pundits thought it fit to hang their petty party accusations on him. Land ownership and use allocation should stay with the governments, whereas actual implementation of projects should be carrotted with the private sector. Government interference in extreme cases has extended to the regulation of personal life including religion (which is quite absurd given its hypno-therapeutic value in managing the social fabric). Pricing should be based on specified rates of return on equity investment. Norms can easily be established for investment per productive resource or per output. In essence, the private sector will 'manage' public resources for a return.

Rights to fundamental physical property should be managed by and should largely reside with the government. For example, the right to own land should be taken away or at best diluted. All land, water and air resources ownership rights should reside only with the government.

Developmental purpose rights may be distributed on revenue sharing basis for limited period of up to 15 years. Financial models should include allocation of development rights (and appreciation) to private interests and payment of rentals to governmental bodies, while retaining all significant ownership with governmental bodies.

Religion:

The presence of religion in society is/was intended as a benevolent influence. Religion as a concept has strong hypno-therapeutic value and helps manage social fabric. Religion is a binding non divisive force.

Religion acquires the attributes of a virulent divisive force only if mixed with politics or even business e.g. when a Church in the USA is run like a business corporation, one can expect un religious like scandals and skeletons. Kept apart from politics, religion functions in a benevolent way, much like the culture of burgers, jeans and fries. It is a health issue, it is a business, it has economics of its own, but is largely benevolent in any form.

The first thing to understand about religion is that religion is a social business, economically speaking. Religion is subject to all the laws of market economics, without exception. The only significant missing component in the structure of religion is that of insurance. Although through a scheme of donor agencies, some religions also provide a form of unemployment and medical insurance.

Indeed there is no reason why religions bodies should not be permitted to list on stock exchanges and raise money through public offerings.

The concepts of religious wars, crusades and persecutions also have their origins in economic necessity. The USA has expanded the inter religions conflict zone to include 'ethnic' violence. The USSR focused on 'propaganda machines', whereas the British and American policies have been to split and dissect society along ethnic and cultural values that are more deeply ingrained, and therefore lead to longer lasting conflicts. The dissection of Yugoslavia, sponsored on both sides by western nations, is a classic example. NATO was effectively used as an instrument to divide and rule and create economically non sustainable 'countries'—really states of European nations. Religious crusades, have long been used by western nations to bring long lasting economic benefits. Hitler attempted to do that, and for a while successfully, however, he took on far more than he could chew, as a result of illogical ambition unsupported by sound strategy. Hitler's forays into Africa and Russia were ill advised as were his alliances with Japan and Italy. Had Hitler not sparred with the USA, today Hitler's Germany would have been alive and well and the USA would have collapsed internally into several different countries under the weight of its many internal inconsistencies. The USA is the Sumo Wrestler of the 21st century, that hard fall to the mat waiting to happen from the adroit kick to the groin by BRICK economies. That is not to say that what happened was a bad thing, being judgmental about history serves little purpose. Questioning, whether, for example, the holocaust actually happened is immaterial. What is material is that the West used the holocaust in the worst possible way—to hurt the Jews again—the West created Israel, to merely collect the Jews in one final destination, to decimate the entire race in one go, and therefore, supports Iran and Iraq in their quest for nuclear weapons.

Palestine-Israel:

The first aspect to recognize is that the conflict in Palestine is not a religious conflict (strangely enough Christians and Jews find themselves on the same side of the wall). It is a business conflict about the allocation of scarce resources. It serves the purpose of Israel, USA and Palestine to keep the conflict going for as long as possible. Therefore, it should be completely ignored from business, economic and religious view points. The conflict has no value, it is in fact a business. This business empire now extends into Lebanon and partly into Iraq. The loss of life is collateral damage and inciden-tal to the furtherance of politico-economic interests. So also in Iraq. Investors in Iraq (there are many) seek higher returns because of the higher risk profile. At any time, there will always exist such high risk-return profile markets e.g Sudan, Ukraine. This is business, this is world commerce. It has been clear for a long time that neither the USA, nor any Western country, nor Jews, nor Palestinian leadership actually want peace. It is currently a lack of Palestinian leadership, as before, that prevents peace. Palestinians cry for a Mandela or a Gandhi (both lawyers by profession) their lawyers, however, prefer to pontificate from the pulpits of the Western press. George Bush, of course, as an oil magnate, couldn't care less if the entire lot were dumped into the Mediterranean (he takes his holidays elsewhere) or were sent up in smoke. Perhaps, to be-gin with, Dr. Rice and team may understand the Middle East situation a tad better, if they did not refer to the Kingdom of Saudi Arabia as 'Soddy' Arabia.

Kashmir-Pakistan–China:

The KPA triangle in the Indian sub continent is of a dif-ferent hue. This area is militarily of strategic importance, or strategically of military importance, I forget which comes first. This conflict is not business—it is strategic in nature. Con-trol over Kashmir provides a road into India—Alexander the Great would tell you that—the road into India made him not so 'great', much like a 25 year old Federer was beaten in an exhibition by a 35 year old Sampras. The conflict for the most part has been financed by China–Pakistan. China has also encroached vast amounts of Indian territory (the state of Arunachal Pradesh is practically under Chinese governance), Tibet, Taiwan etc. These encroachments have strategic im-portance from a military stand point—no commercial utility. Similarly Myanmar (Burma in WW II) is an economic sub set of China, and this too borders India. In the long term, the USA will have to provide military protection to India, simply to thwart Chinese expansion. China through Myanmar, Pakistan and

North Korea of course plans to completely dominate Asia and Africa. China is already in the process of building a super highway into Nepal.

Employment:

Employment is a demographic factor. Employment (level of) is not an economic indicator. A larger number of employed people does not indicate economic health, lower unemployment numbers do not indicate economic development. Higher wage levels are not necessarily a good thing—it may merely indicate a shortage of skilled or unskilled labor in some sectors. What is important is how people are employed, what sectors are they employed in and what is their productivity. Most central banks and ministries of commerce focus on number of employed people and this is the traditional cattle man's approach. People are so many sheep and need to be 'employed' not necessarily gainfully employed—digging ditches is great so long as there is a lunch break in between. This then is the critical fault one sees on visiting the Keynesian ship 2,000 feet at the sea bed. The quality of employment is the only true meaningful index. Is it difficult to compute or monitor. Rather the opposite, it is much simpler than the huge mechanics of monitoring numbers of people seeking employment who do not have jobs (the USA and Europe annually waste an estimate USD 18 to 20 billion only on tracking the score of employment). This wasteful expenditure has a significant economic de multiplier effect. That brings us to the other important issue—employment benefits.

Employment benefits for large classes of humans have a reverse swing effect. i.e. an individual receiving employment benefits has less incentive to work over time as the period of receiving benefits increases—in other words, one actually gets quite easily used to receiving money for not working hardly surprising. Few real benefits are realized from employment doles and from retirement benefits. These two concepts are economic black holes in the economic fabric of nations. Instead governments should provide meaningful employment to individuals who are not able to find work in

the private sector.

The index of meaningful employment is therefore a superior measure of a nation's economic well being. Are people employed in jobs that are commensurate with their skill sets, education and training? Real wage levels are a better indicator of economic health than employment levels.

Poverty levels:

A large amount of time and resources are devoted to understanding how many people are below or above the poverty line. No doubt these resources expended contribute to more people below this imaginary poverty line. The first principle is that the so called poverty line does not exist in reality. This is because it ignores the effect of inflation and the levels of real income growth. It also ignores the effect of concentration of income and this is the killer. Murder by death, as one would say. Of what significance is this indicator? Actually, none. Poverty levels are not national wealth indicators nor even national development indicators. Thus a large number of people below the poverty line could co exist with a really high real gdp growth. This is because quite simply put, everybody is not the Sultan of Brunei or the Queen of Belgium.

Evaluation of projects:

Traditional approaches consider cash flows, payback, internal rate of return, discounted cash flows, net present value, profitability index, earnings per share, price earnings ration, accounting rate of return, return on equity, return on investment, debt coverage etc. These measures are accounting driven and therefore scorecard driven. These approaches do not focus on value and synergy which are in fact the two most important aspects to be evaluated for each potential investment opportunity. What is critical is what value does the project in fact bring to the table. A project that shows net value addition will pay for itself in the long run. A project that pays for itself will have an exit route for investors. Value-cost indicators and maps for each project are essential tools.

The International Monetary Fund and other Fun:

The IMF, humorously referred to (both by contributory and recipient nations) as I (a)m F**ed has been one of the major disasters among economic institutions, much like a ship (never could understand why these are called vessels) that has been steered toward the bottom of the iceberg—this is disaster creation at its very best. The IMF has destroyed economies of under developed countries, created huge indebtedness among both contributors and recipients. The amazing transformation of India from a recipient to a contributor, for example, has nothing to do with IMF policies. In fact, the IMFed cannot showcase a single significant success story throughout its chequered (as in checks written to, not by, developed countries), history. Disappointment has followed disappointment, through a stream of structural recommendations that at best were ill advised and at worst politically motivated. Most IMF policies were designed to create dependent economies and to support the western production giants by providing cheap, stable, dependent export markets (read consuming markets for producers in developed countries). The principal aim of the IMF was essentially to transfer wealth, on a continuous and consistent basis, from developing economies to the developed western economies, notably, France, UK, Italy, Germany and of course the USA. Countries such as Spain, Portugal and Japan, in their position as poor 'relatives' of these countries benefited from the scraps of wealth redistribution. African nations bore the brunt of this massive attack through IPR, globalization and 'free' trade regimes.

Basically, after the disbandment of the Greek, Roman, British, USSR and USA global powers/empires, military ascendancy was no longer seen as an adequate weapon of mass economic destruction. War shifted from an end to a means of economic policy. Territorial expansion was abandoned in favor of economic expansion. Financial dependency relationships were created to support the developed economies. A massive shift of productivity and resources in the late 1990's has resulted in the developed economies now becoming the dependent economies. This is a cyclical shift of both economic and military power. China and India are the next leading economic powerhouses (barring power shortages).

India has little political or geographical expansionist ambitions. China, however, will come to dominate the politico-economic-military scene together with countries such as North Korea, Pakistan and many African and Middle Eastern nations. The period 2010 to 2099 will be marked by Chinese domination of world trade and political equations. Middle Eastern countries will have no option but to ally with China. Countries such as Iran and Iraq will be strong Chinese allies. Israel (not necessarily the Jews) will become increasingly irrelevant, with the diminishing of the economic and military effectiveness of the USA, the United Nations and other Sporting Leagues (of nations) such as the meaningless EU and Commonwealth of nations. The UN has of course, been quite ineffective and a largely 'social' forum for people of different cultures to meet and interact, since the early 1960s. The UN is probably, as a result, the single largest employer of interpreters.

Some unsustainable countries—merge with:

1. Cyprus—Greece
2. S Korea—N Korea—Tibet–Taiwan—China
3. Singapore–Malaysia
4. African nations—one country, one continent as in USA and Australia (see EU example)
5. Bangladesh—Myanmar
6. Bahrain—Iran
7. Kuwait—Iraq
8. Israel—Iraq–Iran
9. Palestine—Lebanon – Syria
10. Armenia, Georgia, Estonia, Lithuania, K-stans—-Russia
11. Mongolia—Tibet–China
12. Singapore/Hong Kong—China
13. Bhutan/Nepal—India/China
14. Pakistan—Afghanistan
15. Sri Lanka—India
16. Canada, Mexico—USA

Israel of course is an artificially, unsustainable State such as Bangladesh, a product of the divide and rule policy of the British. Quite frankly, perhaps the Jews would be far-

happier and trouble free, if they did not have Israel. 'Israel' has brought the Jewish people nothing but a troubled existence and little if any real independence. A truly global

Jewish Diaspora would have been more economically pow-erful. Perhaps the Arabs have a hidden agenda in keeping the Jews weak and cornered by letting them occupy a geo-graphical boundary called 'Israel', especially in the midst of Arab States. For the Jews, it is something like a cobra having a mongoose in the nest.

A Jewish State anywhere else (some, however, will argue that the USA is a true Jewish State) would have become im-measurably economically powerful. Apart from that, most States founded on a religious existence and based on land grabbing, have failed. Zion is hardly the place where the Jews will be 'saved', it is more likely the place where they will be gathered for a final annihilation, surrounded as they are, by their Muslim brethren.

The UN is of extremely doubtful utility and extremely un-convincing, as a body, it resembles a resident of the morgue. Vast waste of resources characterizes the UN. The necessity

of having the UN is highly questionable—most of the aims of the UN remain unachieved and there are little politico-peace gains to speak of. NATO, EU etc. have effectively combined to reduce the UN to an administrative jamboree of wishful inanities. Indeed the entire functioning of the UN has been often likened to a spaghetti western. More so since the instal-lation of Banki Moon. The UN is not a religious body (although in some aspects not unlike the Vatican), not a political, nor economic body. It has no reason to exist. If western powers limit their designs of economic domination, most conflicts will resolve themselves.

Seriously, the UN at its worst has provided the USA with license to invade several countries and lay flag to their economic resources, in the name of furthering democracy.

Democracy:

Democracy is a form of convincing the local populace that they participate in government. That is of course not the case, ever. Politicians govern and businesses govern and, sometimes, military governs. The 'common' man is just that—'common' and does not govern, never will govern. The utility of democracy is highly suspicious. Most democracies would benefit by the addition of a benevolent royal family, if not by the replacement by royal family. What is a 'benevolent' royal family? All royal families dictators are benevolent with few exceptions (prove the rule). Most royal families create an atmosphere of perceived benevolence since this is in their own interests. That is to say, under a dictatorship, or monarchy, one would generally be better off, socially and economically, than under a democracy, provided that one does not object/protest about the monarch or dictator. This actually in practice provides the common man with much more freedom than under a democracy. Why does the West push democracy? Simply because they are afraid of the concentration of resources.

This, then, is the corner stone: DEMOCRACY IS ONLY AN EXTENSION OF THE PRINCIPLE OF DIVIDE AND RULE. In short it is easier for a western power to control a country if it is a democracy—a religious—'Christian' democracy—nobody really likes a 'Hindu' or 'Islamic' democracy. Is the concept of democracy then religious? No, rather is it CRUSADICAL. The term democracy was propounded and advocated by the knights of the crusade, notably, however, the Vatican is not a democratic insitution. It is only due to the vagaries of human nature that 'confession of sins' was not incorporated as a formal institutional pillar of democracy. Big brother is watching and listening and so much the better if you can get people to go and tell Big Brother what they are up to. It was a way of leaving a controllable, predictably legacy. Democracy helped provide economic dependence. A large number of Asian, African and Middle Eastern countries would be far better off economically and socially with a monarchy or at least a dictatorship. A monarchy will usually provide better allocation of resources.

Typically, also, a monarchy provides better generational accountability of resources. The Pharaohs of Egypt lasted that length of time, definitely not because of democratic principles. All the lasting civilizations have been founded on principles other than democratic. In contrast, democracies have had a rather troubled existence and have been short lived. Democracy as a concept, is no more than a couple of hundred years old (and with many more conflicts), whereas, monarchies and dictatorships have provided stability for thousands of years and thousands of years and...... Democracies have resulted in wide spread poverty. It is no secret that SE Asian countries, including India, were enormously wealthy until they became democracies and descended into pits of chaos. Chaos and instability breeds economic poverty—and provides the freedom to be poor and disadvantaged. The Middle Eastern countries will follow the identical fate should they opt for a democratic political system.

One cannot for one moment imagine a democratic Libya, Cuba or Saudi Arabia—the unimaginable chaos is an unthinkable proposition. Iran and Afghanistan are prime examples of countries gone sour with democratic veins hastily transplanted. India is still struggling at the seams and Pakistan wears only a thin cloak of democracy, blown away with every beheading or hanging of a president or prime minister (as is their eventual fate in response to their track record of corrupt, perverted gains).

The most sinister part of democracy is that it is marketed as 'good for your health', with no health warning sub titled. Identical strategies were adopted for marketing SEC type regulations, IMFed type economic policies and of course junk food and soda pop drinks. The master con was to market tap water as bottled 'mineral' water, sold to people who did not trust tap water in many countries. All these were good for people's health. Democracy is the largest social con (and perhaps the most expensive) perpetrated on humankind over the past 5 million years (the other is the wheel—but that is another story—the wheel was not invented—it was always there—as with wings and fire—nobody discovered these things—we take them for granted simply because they always existed and are to be taken for granted—the wheel and fire were given to humans, like the English language.). A billion people in India would testify that they were better off under a Gandhian monarchy. What is a Gandhian monarchy? That is another subject, for another chapter.

International Aid

International aid, today, and for some time, has taken the form of declarations of commitments. It is widely accepted that such commitments often do not materialize to the extent anticipated. Further, aid distribution systems are so poor that only an estimated 3 percent to 4 percent of aid disbursed actually reaches the targeted recipients. International aid should, therefore, take the form, only of transfer of physical and associated human resources, to ensure direct distribution to target population segments. This is the most difficult, least established, yet most effective method of providing international aid. Monetary international aid usually finds its way into personal-political coffers and a bit trickles down into ground reality projects. Perhaps, by far, the best example of support operations that are extremely efficient, are the Mother Teresa homes that provide basic food and shelter and some medical care to the homeless and the dying. The effectiveness of that system is derived from the commitment of those involved in the actual delivery of specific relief measures.

Is aid always relief? Currently, the answer to that is clearly 'NO'. That is a fundamental problem with today's international aid. It usually provides little or no relief of any kind. That is simply because the objectives of most aid programs are not precisely defined (e.g. grandiose motherhood statements such as alleviation of hunger/earthquake affected) and the programs have no distribution support. Thus food for oil programs have been efficiency and corruption disasters. Energy or medical support programs have similarly, been unmitigated disasters—in fact most of these would qualify as disasters, more than the triggering circumstances or incident. Ethiopia, Sudan, Afghanistan, and so many other countries have 'received' plenty of aid, but little relief. The USA has been known to provide a bit of aid with one hand and bomb the place to pieces with the other hand (case in point being Afghanistan, where USA military forces attempt to smash the local population into below the ground submission and categorize nationalists are terrorists or insurgents, similar forces in Kashmir are conveniently called freedom fighters and supplied with aid—stranger—the same forces being bombed as insurgents and terrorists in Afghanistan were armed by the USA when they fought the Russians, and then labeled as freedom fighters).

The other big con is 'humanitarian' aid. Humanitarian aid usually is accompanied by covert religious covenants that compromise the independence of the recipients. Unfortunately, this is one category of aid, wherein, the delivery people are usually taken for a ride as well. Most delivery people sincerely believe that what they are doing is 'noble'. Of course nobody has really defined either 'noble' or 'humanitarian' and so distribution of vaccines that nobody really needs is noble. Is euthanasia 'noble'?. Actually, yes, it qualifies. Is population control 'noble' or humanitarian? Yes, but both will never be focus areas. That is also partly due to the fact that noble, humanitarian causes are supported and sponsored by religious, political, national or business (pharmaceutical companies) causes. In a recent case, humanitarian workers, in a Plooswamy type case, were actually exporting children from an African nation, for adoption, child sex and for body parts, a gruesome business model, if any. In another noted instance, the head of a UN force was routinely seen on global channels, making a case for enhanced relief in Darfur, Sudan. However, it turned out, that those TV interviews were actually the only time the guy ever visited the scene, he was actually using the TV pitches to market himself for a top UN job and also to impress the woman he wanted to marry. The camp residents actually joked about his situation and how he would eagerly, even desperately drum up stories about the camp and shoot extensive TV footage.

What are peacekeeping forces? What was the Indian army doing in Sri Lanka? What are peacekeeping forces doing in Sudan and Lebanon, with or without air support? Nobody really knows. Were the objectives business? Were the objectives political? In fact all UN or other peacekeeping forces have little or absolutely nothing to do with keeping the peace. Political, economic or plain simple trading impulses have sponsored such organized invasions of peace. To compound matters, most peacekeeping forces have 'observer' status and watch sadly as local opposing forces pulverize each other, some peacekeepers are occasionally bumped off as collateral, as in the case of the Jewish invasion of Lebanon. The inactive status of such forces makes them redundant, but not totally so, after all somebody has to keep score.

All international assistance should be government to government sponsored and coordinated and delivered directly by the sponsor. For example, put the blankets, food and other necessities into the hands of the needy—don't deliver to agents who will quickly sell most of it at a profit in the market place. In most earthquake hit areas, the bulk of international aid material is 'freely' available in local market places, sold at discounts to market value.

The Welfare State and Generational Accounting

The current organization of States that are governed democratically, are not 'welfare' oriented. These states do not take into account generational accounting of utilization of resources. For example developed countries have studiously avoided making any meaningful gestures toward the problem of depleting natural resources or global warming.

Ruinous climate, animal and physical resource management policies have resulted in wide spread devastation in most countries. This is because of a lack of commitment to account for resources in terms of the impact on future generations. Country GDP is usually reported without the amortization impact of depleted resources, without accounting for the compromise of future generations' wealth, environment and opportunities.

The current actions of present governments are often dictated by the ages of leaders who are unable and unwilling to look beyond their own lifetimes and in most cases beyond their own terms in Government. Decisions both economic and political, are usually taken not in Gandhian or Mandelian mode, but usually short term. Most political traders have the psyche of stock market traders—and manage their positions session by session. This is the prime reason that strife in most parts of the world, including in the Middle East is programmed to continue to perpetuity.

Natural resources such as land, sea, air, minerals, energy sources, marine life etc. should be properly accounted for, the compromises that nations make, the ravages of economic profiteering, the selling of a country's potential/future should be accounted for, future generations should realize that the comforts of this time, come at the cost of a sadder, less fulfilling future.

Current and future generations should be aware that depleting natural resources are limited in supply and do not regenerate. This is an obvious fact and equally obviously ignored in the election and functioning of governments and economic policy. This is not about global warming, it is a fact that some resources and species are not renewable, now or ever.

Dredging the oceans never really produced more sharks, felling trees never did help discover more tigers and wiping off the whales (by the Japs—this is a wholly irrelevant minor economy still struggling in the after math of WWII, with a limited future and abysmally low concern for human values) only helped along the jelly fish scavengers, not much point in having a resident oceanic delicacy when there is nobody to participate in the feast, ask the salmon and the seals.

Tax Reform

A uniform tax code is clearly required. Much more than a uniform political system, as in the US government's peddling of their warped version of democracy — (space travel is finally here, 'warp' drive has been invented by the West). Fiscal objectives are fundamentally similar — just like chess openings are!! The huge complexity in tax laws are a product (not by product) of bureaucratic work. Bureaucrats need their jobs, so they complicate and create work and the fundamental pillar of this is 'forms' and records. Tax laws and tax rates are designed to require more forms and more records and more justification of lifestyle behavior.

The uniform tax code should be simply based on expenditure. This is easy and simple to design and implement. However, for that very reason, has always received stiff opposition from the 'babus'—the white collared, white eared feather pen pushing men behind the scenes—some of whom eventually find their way into IMF, the World Bank and such other policy pushing institutions, if not various departments of feather bed governmental ministries.

Personal taxation codes are far too complex and time consuming—wasting a huge amount of resources that could otherwise be productive elsewhere—surely the scorekeepers should not be more sophisticated in their knowledge of economic circumstances than the revenue earners?

Basic tax objectives are clear—raise some money for governance and then re distribute some money to reduce at least to some extent inequalities in wealth and income. How difficult is this? Further, should re distribution of wealth be an economic policy objective? Is it not right to have some people richer than others? Can one really have the oppressed without oppression and without the oppressor? Quite simple actually and it really boils down to effectively using a well designed expenditure tax (not these ridiculous sales/vat taxes) that will account for larger and more conspicuous consumption by the relatively wealthy.

Most current tax regimes (tax laws are true regimes—NOT political bosses—this is a classical misuse of the word 'regime' by western powers—in biblical proportions—something like believing the red sea and the dead sea are really red and dead respectively, and then one would have to look for the painter and the murderer, respectively), are based on the following key aspects:

1. Results of operations
2. Status at the end of a period

This does not solve the following:

A   Envy of the relatively poor at the wealthy expanse of the rich midriffs; and

B   Income really results from taxable events—not from results over time, not from going through the motions of living during a taxable year, as a 'resident' of a particular locale (however idyllic).

Thus current tax regimes do not work to re distribute wealth, do not work to reduce basic envy of the relatively economically disadvantaged. The expenditures of the rich would not bother the poor if that expenditure would be taxed and those taxes used to provide benefits to the poor. Simply put, robbing Peter to pay Paul should be institutionalized—this is one of the many opportunities missed by the otherwise excellent Knights Templar (who did a fairly good job with banking in Europe). For example, taxes on a polluter should be more than on a non polluting business, tax a mining rights company more than a transport company, tax a resident occupying (whether by rent or ownership) a plus 2,000 sq.ft house more than a 1,000 sq.ft house, and so on. A zero based approach to tax reform is needed in most countries and this transcends whether the country is endowed with a trillion GDP or otherwise, whether the country is ruled by a dictator or a democratically nominated government (there is no such thing really as a democratically elected government—but that story is told in the *Reverse Merge* together with many more illustrations about parallel universes and business models).

Forecasts

The subject of forecasts occupies a significant amount of time of economists, planners, strategists, business people, financial people and even politicians. Various approaches are used to 'forecast'. Most of these actually yield no meaningful result. A large number of forecasts are based on a study of past trends and then attempts to project that over future periods of time, adjusting for variations in circumstances. Quite often these future variations are inadequate and incorporated into poorly constructed models (financial).

The theory of forecasting clearly therefore, needs revision. If this subject has been downtrodden for centuries yielding

no useful results, then there is something seriously lacking in the development of humankind. Quantum physics and neurosurgery withstanding, this is the biggest black hole in human knowledge. As humans, we were given the wheel, but did nothing with it, other than watch it roll down hill.

The fundamental error that all forecasting models have embedded, is simply that the future can be predicted based on the past. This necessarily implies the following basic erroneous assumptions:

    A. The future is derived from the past
    B. The PRESENT is almost not happening
    C. The future is anytime post the past and does not include the PRESENT e.g. a forecast in 2007 will start with 2008 to say, 2020.

The fact of the matter is really quite different and equally quite simple. The future is largely shaped by the present. This is equally simply because the present, which is happening NOW and HERE, is the future. To fully comprehend this, one should accept that the future exists here and NOW, side by side with the present. One does not need a model or a looking glass to see into the future. The future exists in the present in a marginally different dimension of time and space, but it is here.

Of what use, therefore is the application of forecasts and even worse, projections (based on hypothetical assumptions)? Actually, truth be told, of very little use. The full force of the future is clearly discernible in present actions e.g. you cut a tree today—it wont stand in the future—MOST actions are irreversible in time and space that is the secret of the future impact of the present.

Therefore, should one not act in the PRESENT? On the contrary, the actions of the present build the future, even while one struggles to decipher the future course of events. There is a little linkage to the past, but not much—which is why predictions of movements in stock prices, currency and commodity exchange rates etc. are so lacking in utility. Any true investor will know that present corporate actions determine the future of a corporation and then discount that to account for stock price movements and expectations (an expectation of an event or stream of events is quite different from a prediction/projection/forecast).

There are therefore, no possible scenarios—rather a range of probabilistic estimates that can be constructed based on current actions. Does one estimate or project population? No, personal and governmental actions in the present determine population growth rates—you cannot project or forecast population. What happens tomorrow is a product of today (not so much of the past). This is useful in understanding inflation, employment, housing, currency, even stock price movements. The future exists NOW and HERE. There is no real distinction between THEN and NOW, it is here. All probabilistic estimates are relative to current actions—this is a logical fit with the theory of relativity and Christian science. The trouble and opportunities of tomorrow are here and are being made possible today, the coming of salvation in any form is already here and available for those with faith and confidence– this is not an event or events to happen some time 'later'.

So of what use then is 'looking' into the future? This is a bit of a circumendrum. The actions of the present are sought to be planned on the basis of expectations of the future, but the actions of the present actually determine the future. Is the future therefore, entirely controllable? The broadest sense of business or political environment is not (bye the way, try telling that to the Jews) controllable, it is in fact uncontrollably dynamic and spoilt by the fallibilities of human nature.

However, it is a bit like steering a raft through troubled waters. Can one determine the direction of the river, the rapids, the height of the waterfall? Hardly, to even imagine the capability to do so would be fool hardy in the extreme. BUT, BUT take stock for a moment, how you handle the spears (I hate calling them oars—this is a very limited calling and definition) actually determines how you handle the waterfall and the course. Does the experienced rafter change his handling based on how he thinks he will hit the waterfall? I think not, it is quite the other way around.

It is a cheery thought, that, while you plan for the future, you are already in the future and determining the future, it exists now. If every student for an examination believed in this truism, there wouldn't be any failures, only successful candidates or drop outs. Too many generals fight their wars of the future with the results of wars of the past.

Small Business Enterprises

Small business enterprises, for the purposes of this discussion, includes mom'n'pop, pop'n,mom, pop'n'pop. 's(h)op and pop' and family managed businesses (not purely family owned).

Family businesses deserve special economic attention. The economic wheels, spokes, what have you, inflation, employment, currency etc. are heavily impacted by the health of the family business—trading, gas stations, groceries, services, agencies, small scale manufacturing (has a humungous economic multiplier effect—to stimulate the economy, stimulate small scale manufacturing). The success of India and China is largely due to the heavy support and focus by governmental bodies, agencies and lending institutions on supporting small scale enterprise. The Small Scale industrial banks of India did a whopping job of financing family businesses. Family businesses create real, genuine, 24 carat value (and by that logic should also be given tax breaks).

BIG secret. The reason they do create such value is because they are not focused on shareholder value through stock market prices—they are focused on wealth creation through generation of CASH surplus. CASH is king in the family business and the successful venture is typically a result of a sound business model and excellent cash management (cost control, financing facilities, internal controls, inventory management). CASH measures value addition and value delivery. The discussion below deals with some dynamics of family businesses. A note of caution—the reader here, could find a marginal disconnect in writing style—this is a result of the fact that some of the related theoretics and research was developed years before the current volume was put together—the author, however, is the same, yours truly, just from a different time and space, rather than from the NOW, before the tales of MEOWs were developed and put to paper (to do that the author had to go up into the mountains and ….eat). Cash, cash and DAILY cash flows run family businesses. This stimulates development, cost management and innovation. Family businesses are largely unaffected by the sickness of chasing stock market indices (illusionary economic wealth).

The secret of a vibrant economy is innovation, innovation in marketing, packaging, distribution and product development. The small business is often more in touch, in tune with market needs, more direct contact translates into a better understanding of market needs. The small business IS the market, not just in the market. The small business represents the modular approach to sound economic management.

Commitment to the success of the business is also far greater in the average small business. This is because large corporations *employ* personnel, personnel who rarely assume ownership, often personnel have to be taught to take 'ownership'. In small/family businesses, ownership is a natural characteristic—e.g. you don't have to teach a leopard aggression. Ownership is ab initio, off the blocks, cartwheeling around throughout the psyche of the small business.

It is critical for a country, to keep the small business ticking over. A clear indicator of economic ill health is failing small businesses, family ventures that cannot meet their commitments to the banks, family businesses that cannot find the capital to expand operations regionally or vertically (again using the compact modular business approach will limit size to manageable proportions). The author as management consultant has often struggled to break down and break up, family businesses into smaller manageable strategic business units—size is often not an advantage in terms of ownership and equity capital, unless it is applied to centralized purchasing for distributed operations. Outsourcing of decentralized and non core functions plays a key role in this process of managing modular growth.

Nature:

Family businesses are pervasive and constitute the vast majority of businesses worldwide. A common misconception is that family businesses are small to medium in size. However, several family businesses in Kuwait and globally are large. e.g. Wal—Mart with annual revenues in excess of USD 150 billion is a family businesses. Other family firms include Johnson & Johnson, DuPont, Liz Clairborne . Best estimates show that in the United States, between 50% to 60% of all public companies are family controlled. In a country such as India, the Tata, Birla, Ambani (Reliance), Mittal, Ruia (Essar), Vedaanta/Sterlite (Agarwal), Wadia, Infosys, Wipro, Chhabria (to name a few and not necessarily in that order) all started out as family businesses and have remained so in many aspects. The corresponding percentage for Kuwait is clearly much higher as a result of the close demographics of the Kuwaiti society. Family businesses combine two almost opposing aspects of businesses—namely, performance based management and emotion based positional domination of the control structure.

Family businesses can fall into one of several categories. Family owned, family managed, family controlled and family effective (owned, controlled and managed). The operational classification depends upon the degree of participative management that the owners desire and are capable of exercising. Capability to exercise ownership is a factor of the degree of ownership and to a larger extent, very often, the degree of historical participation in day to day management.

For example an ownership group that has seldom seen the inners of the company, would find it extremely difficult to attempt to exercise management control in the event of a succession challenge (death of a key member) or in the event of change in the structure of the company—say, listing the company on a stock exchange or implementing a formal mechanism of corporate governance.

Two Family Concept:

In several countries, many family owned businesses in reality have two 'families'. One, being the family that owns the majority equity and another being the family that runs the company (i.e. the investing family and the managing family). The management family invariably, is more characterized by dynastic control and nurturing of descendant family members, whereas, the investing family is characterized by nurturing of *ascendant* family members. The risk of the presence of the management family (as contra distinguished from the owner family) is that the management family, over time and over generations acquires a shareholding stake and then begins to exercise effective control at the board level in addition to the day to day operations. With the passage of time, the owner family takes an increasingly back seat role. The owner family members are then likened to a passenger in the back seat of a car giving driving instructions to another passenger (possibly a board member) in the front seat of the car, while looking out of the rear window. In reality, of course, the driver is somebody else and neither passenger is fully cognitive of the fact.

Risk Management:

The essential risks of family managed businesses are the risks of inadequate:

- Succession planning
- Devolution of equity shareholding through generations by design or otherwise (as in cases where there is no 'will')
- Separation of ownership from management
- Delegation of authority
- Clear accountability for success and clear definition of what constitutes ' success'
- Definition of the uniform business strategy and business model; and
- Responsibility of various stakeholders to add value in their own individual undiminished capacities.

Succession planning of both equity ownership and management roles are equally important. Unplanned devolution of either equity ownership or management control, through the death of a family member, often causes all round hardship and dynamic chaos that may take another generation to resolve, if the business actively survives the turbulence. Succession planning and devolution needs should be carefully examined and monitored in the interests of good relationships and smooth functioning. Large family businesses indeed would benefit from a system of Generational Accounting.

Generational Accounting in the context of family businesses would involve a careful consideration of the impact of equity and control transactions in the context of the impact of these transactions on future generations of the ownership and management structure. For example a transfer of equity shares outside the family could have serious long term implications for the family, this is a possibility if the stock is listed and publicly traded. Similarly the development of a professional second line in key positions (e.g. CEO/COO/MD) could have long term implications on the management 'family's' control structure.

Often the discordant note at the highest level is in terms of strategic interest and in terms of what constitutes success. For the equity owners who will hold on to their stock, success would be defined by profitability, cash inflows, growth of the business and dividend returns. For equity owners who will divest in time, success would be defined in terms of listing on stock exchanges where they will have a better price—earnings ratio and market capitalization, better overall liquidity. For management family members, success could mean the employment of more family members in key positions, the expansion of the corporate structure into divisions/strategic business units/subsidiaries/associates together with minor shareholdings in each of these group units. The management family members could access shares through share awards, purchase shares from the market, purchase shares from other 'family' shareholders, employee stock option schemes etc.

Limitations of Perceived Capabilities
(and perceived limitations of capabilities):

The business strategy and business model in most instances is a factor of the owner—management groups' perception of their limitations. The prime moving strategic target is to protect their cash flow interests. Most family groups, whether owner or management, will therefore, strive to function within their perception of their own limitations. This stems from their desire to retain control and achieve their growth objectives within an environment that is familiar to them and entirely within their capabilities to manage. Some family businesses have therefore, benefited from successive generations abilities to acquire, through education and training, new capabilities. The business then has confidently and without the insecurities of loss of control, grown in new directions.

Family owned and managed businesses are therefore strongly characterized by a streak of insecurity and the de-sire to limit business operations to functional and financial capacities and limitations. Either or both functional and finan-cial parameters may alter with incremental efforts or in some instances just pure good fortune!! supported by shrewd busi-ness instinct.

Accountability is quite another story. Accountability in most companies is like the delightful rabbit in the forest or the chicken in the yard, always seen and rarely in hand. However, surprisingly, accountability lines are much better drawn in family owned—managed businesses. This is because accountability in family owned—managed businesses is usually carefully balanced with the delegation of risk taking rights ('RTRs')and with the pattern of financial contributions and the rights to earn financial returns (interest on loans and dividends on equity). Such a neat balancing act between RTRs, financial returns on one hand and accountability on the other hand is usually achieved over time and careful nudging. Historical experience in terms of financial and operational management and risk taking abilities helps a good deal. Some owner groups are for example, clearly better in a passive, even altruistic, public image role. Whereas others are better in behind the scenes operations management.

Managing the Value Proposition:

The management of the business value proposition is another challenge. The distribution of the responsibility to man-

age and enhance the value proposition in a competitive environment, should take into account individual abilities to contribute effectively on a professional level. For the success of the business, roles for family members should ideally not be carved from professional responsibilities. There are roles for professional managers and guiding roles for family members. Family members could set the implementation framework for the chosen strategic direction, code of conduct and ethics. Family members should have a degree of affinity of interest that stretches beyond the most committed, stock option plan driven professional manager.

The family member often has a far better realization of the value of business assets, both tangible and intangible, simply because s/he has been in close proximity to the degree of personal effort and risk that has contributed to the development of the business assets. This proximity of a risk taking entrepreneur, to the process of asset acquisition, stretches beyond that of the best professional manager, a fact that most professional managers are loathe to admit. Equity risk taking is the most serious business of putting your money where your mouth is. Then leveraging that to include others' equity and loan funds creates an altogether different risk, especially in a relatively small economic environment as in the State of Kuwait.

Reputational risk ('RR'):

RR is every entrepreneurial family's nightmare and perennial limiting factor. Most families will not expand a business operation despite well presented rates of return, because of the relatively high RR, that stems from entering a potentially high risk venture or from entering an operational arena about which family members have comparatively low knowledge levels and therefore diminished capacities to create a successful business model. Functional and financial limitations come together in a cascade and are molded into RR to apply the breaks to entrepreneurial spirit in a family owned—managed business. RR also has a direct and material impact on growth capacity.

Structurals:

The structure and the organized scheme of things differs substantially in family effected businesses. The family effected business does not follow the traditional pattern of the top—down level based box type structure. This is because of the dynamics of positional and emotional authority, parental and sibling authority, both implied and explicit.

The most usually observed structural pattern follows the oldest system in the universe. That of the planetary system. The head of the family being the 'sun' and the other family members being at varying orbits . (distances) to the 'sun'. Another similarity on the lighter side, is that some family systems have un discovered or late discovered planetary members!! The structures of a solar system (sun, planets and satellites) can easily explain the dynamics of the family effected business and can be well integrated into the concept of generational accounting, in terms of assessing generational impact of family decisions. Comet-like risks at times, ravage family businesses, as they do all solar systems.

Structurals of family businesses are often overly stressed due to inadequate levels of communication. Another important stress factor in the constant focus of the members in charge of operations, on current needs (their lifetime needs). Lifetime needs based decisions could have serious generational accounting financial and structural impacts. Family businesses should have the boldness to borrow/purchase vision and mission statements, goals and strategic objectives, from professional managers and consultants if necessary. Recognition must be explicit that all resources do not necessarily reside within the family and the acquisition of managerial or strategic resources does not necessarily come with dilution of equity.

A lack of a proper governance structure is a key factor that prevents most family effected businesses in developing countries, from adding value beyond the third generation. The solar structure should be recognized explicitly. There is a need to continually renew and at some stage replace the founder's drive. This is necessary to cope with a rapidly growing environment, both in competitive terms and in terms of technological scope of development. The diversification of nurtured assets is an important task that can be achieved structurally, through the assignment of roles. Some family member may be rested to pasture, being beyond their prime, whereas others may be moved in the driver's seat for new acquisitions and for balancing the portfolio. A multiplicity of business interests is in fact often indicated as essential, to avoid a situation where all family members hang on to the existing business, until the tilt accommodates and indeed drives the first waters of failure into the ship.

The nurturing of knowledge and intellectual capital are other important tasks for a family effected business. The generational transfer of knowledge and intellectual assets, willfully and actively will ensure continuity of development and movement up the maturity curve.

The Valuation of Countries

Why is the valuation of countries important? Why is the valuation of countries even more important than reporting exports, GDP, real GDP, currency or gold reserves? The answer is that historical accounting is like a bad detective (novel) who (that) actually explains nothing while boring everybody with a large final, meandering chapter that desperately seeks to find some meaning to the awful story line. Notice that in my own short renderings in this book, I have cut the chase directly to the last chapter—the revelations—no point in sniffing non existent roses along the way.

So, how is the economic health of a country typically reported? GDP, real GDP, inflation, employment, gold reserves, currency reserves, currency exchange rate, exports-imports and population. For some specific countries and regions, oil & gas production, software exports are thrown in for good (or bad) measure. None of these measures really tell us what is happening in the country, much less what will happen in the country. For e.g. the sub prime collapse and the see—saw movements of the Asian stock markets were just not 'covered' by such analytics (I cant see stock markets any other way—they are either children's see-saws or high swings—you go WHEEE up and then WHEEE down, depending upon the weight behind the push or the weight at the other end).

The following key factors are not taken into account when evaluating or even assessing snapshot economic progress:

- Inflow of foreign funds (whether stock market or real estate)
- Changes in levels of domestic production and consumption
- Utilization of mineral resources
- Military expenditure
- Expenditure on democratic institutions
- Research and development expenditure
- Success in sporting events (a key viable alternative to waging war, akin to the 'duel' concept of old, albeit with less drastic results)
- Expenditure on arts, cultural activities, sports, music

Models for evaluation of the progress of economies, popularly used by institutions, focus on evaluation rather than valuation. Economies cannot be subject to coarse 'evaluations', they can in fact only be valued at a point in time and these point comparisons can be reviewed as they develop, to ascertain whether progress is being made in the desired direction.

The starting point for the valuation of an economy is GDP. Preferably, one should use nominal GDP not real GDP or inflation adjusted GDP. Even more preferred is the approach to disregard country specific geographical boundaries and consider regional GDP. One should never forget that geographical boundaries that are country specific are artificial in every way and that these boundaries are not useful in any way to understand and review economic progress. For example, the Middle East, South East Asia and North America are one economic unit, as are South America, Western Europe and Eastern Europe (there is really no such thing as a country, Commonwealth of Nations, EU etc. from a pure economic perspective)

Japan and Australia are perhaps the only two significant economic entities that stand alone (again I would not include Norway or Cyprus), some would argue that Egypt should be included in the Middle East, but that is neither here nor there, since historically it is an African nation.

Israel of course is an artificially, un sustainable State such as Bangladesh, a product of the divide and rule policy of the British. Quite frankly, perhaps the Jews would be far happier and trouble free, if they did not have Israel.

So, the regional economic unit valuation should be as follows:

A. Real GDP
B. Less: Foreign direct investment
C. Less: Expenditure on democratic governmental institutions and elections
D. Less: Military expenditure
E. Less: Excess of imports over exports
F. Less: Value of domestic consumption of mineral resources
G. Less: 5% of GDP if quality of available water and other natural resources (e.g. forests) has fallen (most countries will be liable for this 5% deduction).
H. Less: 5% to 15% of GDP for corruption related payments within the country.
I. Add: Research and development expenditure
J. Add: Welfare expenditure including government expenditure for the elderly, children, common facilities etc.
K. Add: Expenditure on infrastructure (roads, bridges, railways, airports)
L. Add: Expenditure on arts, cultural activities, sports and music
M. Add: Increase in domestic production over the previous year (valued at current prices—not inflation indexed)
N. Add: Increase in average market capitalization over previous year

O. Add: Increase in average value of currency relative to the dollar over the previous year
P. Add: Increase in US dollar reserves
Q. Add: Increase in gold reserves
R. Add: Value of increase in known mineral reserves
S. Add: $500 X increase in number of people earning more than $100,000 per year.

'Country' above refers to a group of related countries/regions (regional economic unit) e.g. South East Asia, Korean peninsula, Africa, Middle East, Western Europe including UK, North America, South America etc.

The above is designed to provide a snapshot 'health check' by bringing focus to meaningful parameters of economic and human development. The recommended framework, however, will retain validity only so long as the US dollar remains an international currency i.e. for the next 12 years or so, before the gold standard or the oil standard (*the energy standard*) returns. The energy standard will reflect reserves of both conventional and non conventional energy, thus countries such as Brazil, India and Russia will have huge 'currency' reserves that will fundamentally support their sustained economic growth.

The use of a predictive economic regional valuation model will help predict why some regions will do better economically speaking than others. For example, even a very high level valuation will show that the African continent has by far the best potential going into the 22nd century. Northern America and Europe are essentially spent forces (sic—over spending and borrowing), whereas, South East Asia will continue to struggle with problems of the huge population and health care issues.

The Author

Savio Sebastian Gomes is a Roman Catholic, Goan-Maharastrian, Indian, Mumbaite, Bandraite. He did his early schooling in a Jesuit institution, St. Stanislaus High School. He has lived and worked in India (over 12 cities), Kuwait, and Saudi Arabia (Jeddah). He has also worked on professional projects ('assignments') in the USA (San Jose), UK, Australia (Tasmania and Thalanga), Armenia (Yerawan), Kenya (El Doret and Nairobi), Iran (Tehran), UAE (Dubai and Abu Dhabi), Bahrain and has traveled to Thailand (Bangkok), Sultanate of Oman, Qatar (Doha), Singapore, Toronto, Chicago, Houston, Boston, New York, Denver, Perth, Melbourne, Brisbane, Burnie and Queenstown.

He qualified as a Chartered Accountant in May 1988, Bachelor's of Commerce in 1982 and as a Certified Internal Auditor in 1996, Masters of Commerce in 1999, Doctorate in strategic studies in 2002, and has since then, worked functionally (actually frantically) as an auditor, financial accountant, internal auditor, management auditor, profitability improvement—cost reduction specialist, consulting dot com CEO, transaction support consultant, business advisory services consultant, organization re structuring consultant, and corporate finance (direct investments) professional. He has worked on projects in a large number of industries, with many entrepreneurs, both small scale and large corporate enterprises. His work on valuation of intangibles, privatization, valuation of dot.com, development of family owned businesses, macro economic development and employee ownership of corporations is path breaking.

He has worked on strategic advisory projects for corporations and firms in industries and sectors such as shipping (commercial carrier), aviation (low cost and full service carriers), copper mining, telecom manufacturing, telecom services (mobile operator), steel (large scale integrated steel plants), pharmaceuticals (including formulations, bulk drugs and third party manufacturing), chemicals, small scale engineering manufacturing, large scale engineering manufacturing, ferro alloys, textiles, polyester yarn, turf club (horse racing club), real estate, investments, banking, retail clothing, retail food, cement, healthcare, and consumer finance among others.

Savio started working at the age of 15 (at the time of writing, has been working for 30 years with around 60 days of leave between 1999 and 2007 over a period of 8 years, thus averaging around 7.5 days leave per calendar year) and has worked through his professional studies in various jobs as a part time accountant in hotels and restaurants (cashier, bar cashier, payroll accountant, accountant). During his professional career he worked as a Director (with two big 4 audit-consulting firms), Associate Partner and Partner—Management Consultancy. He is also a chess enthusiast, has two cats (had a beautiful dog for over 15 years), follows tennis and cricket, enjoys walking and cycling. He has been living and working in Kuwait since 2002. Savio is now 45 and pursuing new creative avenues, including some of the fictional works referred to in this book. His experiences are real, when he writes about a country, it is there, when he writes about a city, it is there, when he writes about the ten blunders of economic development, they are there, now and in the future.